Coinage of the Americas Conference

Proceedings No. 2

America's Currency
1789-1866

Coinage of the Americas Conference
at The American Numismatic Society, New York

October 31 - November 2, 1985

ISSN 8756-6265
ISBN 0-89722-213-K

Illustrations of numismatic objects are all reduced except the following which are actual size: pp. 54, 99, 100, 101, 102, 133.

All illustrations are ANS except: pp. 30-46, 66, 84 (fig. 3), courtesy of the Smithsonian Institution, DC; p. 82, courtesy of the New York Public Library; p. 84 (fig. 2), courtesy of The Henry Francis du Pont Winterthur Museum; p. 86, courtesy of the Metropolitan Museum of Art (gift of the estate of James H. Hyde, 1959); pp. 62, 63, 67, 76, 87, 88, 90-93, 97, 99-103, 105, 107, 109, 1110, 117, 118, 122-25, 131-33, 141, courtesy of the author.

Printed in the United States of America

Contents

Preface

Every worthwhile project begins with someone's good idea. Harry W. Bass, Jr., President of the American Numismatic Society from 1978 until 1984, outlined his concept of an ongoing conference series on specialized topics in American numismatics at the Society's 125th anniversary celebration in the fall of 1983. One year later, the first Coinage of the Americas Conference became a reality.

The purpose of these conferences is to facilitate the exchange of information. Toward this end, experts in the field are invited to present papers, collectors are invited to exhibit, and notice of the conference is circulated widely to encourage attendance by all interested in the topic. The Society also mounts an exhibition from its holdings and invites registrants to come to know the Society's collections and library better during the days of the conference. This invitation was best expressed by Society President Harry W. Fowler in his opening remarks to the 1985 Conference. "Our hope and our expectation is that the exchange of ideas this weekend will give impetus to a wider use of the great resources here at the Society and enhance cooperation among all of us in the study and elucidation of these historical artifacts."

Contributors

The Society is grateful to the following contributors who helped make this conference possible:

Richard J. Balbaton
Dorothy Budd Bartle
Elvira Clain-Stefanelli
Bertran M. Cohen
John P. Donoghue
Kenneth L. Edlow
Dr. and Mrs. George E. Ewing, Jr.
Dr. Jay M. Galst
David Ganz
Cory Gillilland
Philip A. Kominos
Joseph R. Lasser
Allen F. Lovejoy
Emmett McDonald
R. Henry Norweb, Jr.
Jules Reiver
P. Scott Rubin
Raphael E. Solomon
Raymond M. Waltz
Barry Wexler

The Professional Numismatists Guild

Introduction

Presented herein are the papers delivered at the second annual Coinage of the Americas Conference. It is apparent from the diversity of topics that the currency of early America is an incredibly rich field. Roger Durand's paper introduced us to the entire area, discussing why private notes should have made their appearance when they did, how they changed through time, and why they finally disappeared from the scene. And even from this introduction, we see that America's early currency might prove interesting in a variety of fields.

As Evira Clain-Stefanelli points out, there's much material here for the American historian. She has called the early bank note "a mirror of life in the early Republic." And so it is: by examining it closely, we can see ourselves as we once were. We can see how we earned our living, what we considered beautiful, how we viewed our nation. In the absence of photographs, the obsolete note is perhaps our best window on the past.

It is the charm and historic importance of these early notes which attracted collectors in the past. As Grover Criswell sees it, there is a good deal more to the present attractiveness of the obsolete note than simple artistry: this currency represents an excellent investment opportunity, and will continue to do so in the future. And so the private note is finally likely to receive the attention it deserves from the collector.

Paper currency of this era can also be used to illustrate the development of ideas and themes, as Gene Hessler has shown us. We see the changing ways in which a single image, that of America as an Indian princess, was handled by the early engravers of our paper currency: it is a theme which goes back to the Discovery itself in some ways, and it reached its apogee on coinage with Saint-Gaudens's magnificent (and totally unrepresentative) Indian on the eagles of 1907-1933.

The artistry concerning our early money may impress us for its own sake. Glenn Jackson has chronicled the fortunes of a truly amazing family of bank note artists, the Smillies, whose labors outlasted the obsolete note itself, providing us with some of the most enduring, best-known images in our national numismatic repertoire.

Of course, the primary purpose of the medium was not to teach, to spread ideas, to move us with its artistry, but to circulate as money, ordinarily at a time when "hard" money—coinage—was in short supply or lacking altogether. We must always bear in mind that the reason for the presence of *any* form of paper currency in nineteenth-century America was the absence of that which would really have been preferred, gold and silver coins, which was based in turn on a scarcity of those precious metals until rather late in the period. Lacking them, and the coins which might have been created from them, the people turned to paper.

The federal government would have little say in the production of the medium for many years, due to lingering fears of a second monetary collapse mirroring the first one, at the time of the American War for Independence. Instead, others would be called upon to produce our currency. Eric Newman takes us back to a very early emergency situation, brought about by the War of 1812, when New York City issued its own small change notes. Mr. Newman's paper was adapted for presentation at the Conference by Joseph R. Lasser; we are grateful to Mr. Lasser for this courtesy and for leading the lively discussion which followed.

The entrance of a public authority into note production, as in the New York City case underscores the unusual gravity of the situation: in most instances, including emergency ones, private issuers would provide our money. Robert Vlack's paper bears this out, focusing on a later period of fiscal crisis, the 1830s and early 1840s. Andrew Jackson's War against the Second Bank of the United States helped create a banking panic and one of the worst economic depressions in our history, and the money which was printed at the time, much of it of an emergency character, faithfully reflects the economic turbulence of those days. These notes, and the economic troubles which brought them into being, serve to remind us of paper's essential fragility as a circulating medium.

Cory Gillilland examines a slightly later period, the 1840s. She concentrates on how paper money actually functioned and circulated in the economic marketplace at that time. Again, we are reminded that this currency was produced, not for the historian and not for the collector, but rather for those who wished to buy something, to sell something else. Her inclusion of actual daily information from that era added a new, important dimension to the Conference.

Paper currency built the factories, railroads, canals and cities of nineteenth-century America. It provided the capital essential for the continued growth of a dynamic young Republic. To paraphrase Voltaire, if the concept of paper money had not existed, it would have had to be invented. Paper could also be employed to expand the limits of government beyond customary boundaries. To the point in this country, it could be used to fight wars.

When the Southern portion of the United States elected to separate from the remainder of the country in the spring of 1861, it decided to finance its war of independence by the issue of paper currency. Chronically short of specie, the Confederacy had no other choice in the matter. The currency came in various forms.Carl Carlson describes the links between the issuers of the old, pre-war private notes and the new national currency endangered by the conflict. These links were close: The fortunes of Southern bankers would rise or fall with the fortunes of the Southern Confederacy itself.

Douglas Ball discusses the tribulations endured by the Confederate Treasury Department, faced with a dearth of decent security printers, shortages of paper and ink, and problems with counterfeiting. All of these led to a reform of currency design in 1862, which would essentially carry the aspiring nation to the close of the war—and to its own demise.

Finally, Raymond Williamson reminds us that, in many ways, the Civil War was a local war, going on simultaneously in many places and causing fiscal strains in many localities. The towns and cities in the North and South, the merchants and county governments, met the war's challenge as best they could; and, in the absence of orthodox money (which had gone underground at the approach of trouble), they printed *un*orthodox money of their own. Mr. Williamson devotes his attention to his own town, Lynchburg, Virginia, but what he reports here could be duplicated in a thousand other places,

North and South.

The end of the war brought the end of the purely private note, and, of course, the demise of the Confederate and Southern States notes as well. In essence, individuality was exchanged for conformity, for centralized control, for a more biddable currency backed by a single authority, the federal government. The old system had demonstrated its inadequacy at the time of the war, and it was not reinstated at its end. All that remain from the previous era are a few of the notes themselves, colorful reminders of who we were, what we did, how we lived and viewed life in an earlier age.

Richard G. Doty
Conference Chairman

The Confederate Currency Reform of 1862

Douglas B. Ball

Coinage of the Americas Conference
at The American Numismatic Society, New York

In the summer and fall of 1862, the Confederate Treasury Department faced a whole series of crises; crises, one might note, that were to a considerable degree of the Secretary's own making. By failing to prod Congress vigorously in the matter of taxation either during the Provisional Congress or during the opening session of the First Regular Congress, Secretary Christopher G. Memminger had guaranteed the absence of fiscal revenues and permitted the Congress to place the whole burden of supporting the war on the monetary side of the Treasury. And since even Secretary Memminger was well aware that a plantation economy had only a limited lending capacity, particularly if its crops could not be sold (as was the case from 1861 on); this meant in turn that all expenses would have to be met by the use of a government currency.

But for probably the first time in history, a goverment hellbent on a printing press economy was hindered in its goals by the absence of the printing personnel and materials needed for that purpose. Henry D. Capers, Chief Clerk of the Treasury Department during the Provisional Government and Memminger's biographer, pointed out with only slight exaggeration that there was only one security engraving establishment in the whole South, consisting of a small shop manned by one engraver, his young son, and an assistant (the American Bank Note branch in New Orleans, which masqueraded during its Confederate period under the adopted firm name, Southern Bank Note Company). The reality, though, was bad enough with only three engravers and half a dozen lithographers, together with the typeset capacity available to the firm of Evans & Cogswell in Charleston.

These ludicrously inadequate resources, not all of which were available to the government, obviously had to be augmented and were—with imported talent, materials and the inducement of various non-printing oriented businessmen to take in hand the task of organizing and operating securities printing firms. Unfortunately, numerous blunders were made in this ad hoc approach to the problem, fundamentally attributable to Secretary Memminger's undisguised laissez-faire beliefs and his hard money view that the treasury notes could and would be dispensed with after the war as a means of public finance. As shall be shortly seen, others more perspicacious than he, watching the growing tidal wave of "Memminger's Gigantic Skunk Cabbage" otherwise known as the Confederate currency, had come to a different view without ever being able to convince the Secretary of the error of his ways. The Secretary's attitude found its most pernicious expression in his refusal to regulate the activities of those who, because of the capital, materials and manpower furnished to them by the government, were little better than extensions of the Treasury. As a result, no permanent arrangements were made—contracts let printers use Confederate resources for the manufacture of rival state, bank and private currencies while less profitable Treasury orders were left unfilled.

Equally undesirable was a whole train of other evils. Without adequate supervision, printers multiplied the number of designs for each denomination, thereby promoting confusion and making the work of even the most inept counterfeiters easy. Moreover, too many high denomination notes had to be printed to meet the Treasury's needs thereby dislocating the currency. And above all, the competition which the Secretary promoted in the interest of trying to reduce the printing bills (regulating the production of unnecessary plates would have been more to the point of getting rid of bill padding) only resulted in cut-throat maneuvers in which the stealing of one another's workmen, arson, interception of rivals' supplies and elaborate intrigues, not excluding trumped-up treason charges, wasted the time and energies of all concerned, while hundreds of thousands of soldiers deserted the Confederate Army for the lack of food, clothing, arms, shelter and pay, because of an empty Treasury.

These cancers in the Confederate financial program (if it can be honored with such a name), reached acute form in the summer and fall of 1862 because of two factors which might have been reasonably anticipated. First, there was a striking need to reduce the currency to manageable size by a forced funding program. This meant that the printers would have to print a large quantity of bonds which would divert them and their limited printing capabilities away from the currency, itself urgently needed to pay past and present bills. Then, thanks to a group now known as the Payne brothers, Yankee intruders penetrated into the South where they distributed nearly $2 million of counterfeit money, thereby causing the public to refuse to receive nearly $150 million of notes printed by the firm of Hoyer and Ludwig. Thus the government had to catch up on $50 million of arrears, clear off a minimum of $150 million of discredited currency plus another $100 million which needed funding, together with the bonds into which these were to be funded, plus produce the $40-$50 million per month needed to meet current needs. And all this new currency clearly needed to be of better quality than the earlier issues to avoid the counterfeiting panic which then engulfed the country.

It was obvious therefore that there were going to have to be radical changes in the way the Treasury produced its secursitites, the designs of the currency and the relations between the printers and the Treasury. Equally, the Treasury was going to have to tackle the in-house bottlenecks which were also a contributory factor in this vexatious equation.

Characteristically, the Secretary chose to address himself to these last first. Among the most pressing of these was the delay imposed on getting currency and bonds out—each note was autograph signed by clerks, each bond was signed by the Register and each coupon was signed by one of his clerks. The United States and the Confederacy had both faced this problem in mid-1861 when the Treasurers and Registers on both sides had been relieved of the duty of signing all notes personally. This had been carried one step further in February 1862 when the United States legal tender legislation allowed printed signatures. The Treasury, by way of precaution, printed the Treasury seal on every note not printed by the Bureau of Engraving and Printing, which had been established with a view to getting out Government securities without the aid of banknote firms whose self-interest made them suspect in Washington.

If signing notes by hand was speedily discarded in comparatively manpower-rich Washington, continuing such practice in Richmond was sheer folly. Fortunately, the Union invasions had created quite a number of refugees and Secretary Memminger had availed himself of the work force thus unintentionally furnished him to hire a corps of women who performed these duties while male clerks were diverted to more important tasks or shipped off to the army. However, this system did not always work well as the work force was not used to keeping business hours, while sickness and "female complaints" etc., left the signing forces out of balance (notes signed by one person each from the Treasurer's or Register's division) or short by one designated partner or another. Printed signatures, which the Congress had not heretofore seen fit to authorize, were a clear necessity.

Accordingly, Secretary Memminger wrote in July 1862 to the Chief Clerk of the Treasury Note Bureau in Columbia, Joseph D. Pope, asking him to sound out the printers on the feasibility of using printed signatures. On July 31, Edward Keatinge, on behalf of the his firm, Keatinge & Ball, replied, advising the use of printed signatures with the same precautions used in Washington, that is, the application of a seal to each note, before issue, and without which the note would be invalid.[1] The Secretary duly petitioned the Congress for the necessary legislation, but with the exception of the 50 cent notes authorized by the an act in April of 1863 (and later the bond coupons), such permission was never forthcoming. Thus the Treasury would have to struggle on until the end of the war with clerks signing $1 and $2 bills worth perhaps 2-5 cents in coin.

The next question was what to do about the relations between the Treasury and its recalcitrant contractors. Fortunately, a series of events transpired in 1862 which offered new opportunities to anyone with the wisdom and vigor to exploit them. The most important of these was the providential arrival in the South, aboard the *Giraffe*, of a crew of 20 Scottish lithographers whose services had been contracted for in London, on behalf of the Confederacy, by Major Benjamin Ficklin, Quartermaster General of the Commonwealth of Virginia. Ficklin, who had been in London to procure military supplies for Virginia, had undertaken the additional commission of hiring printers and did so. The printers had been contracted for on two very specific terms; first they were to be paid £4 a week in coin and second, they were to work exclusively for the Treasury and not for any private contractor or any person engaged in the printing business for profit. These terms were almost made to order since had the Secretary the mind to do so, he had the nucleus with which to set up a Confederate Bureau of Engraving and Printing. It would then have been a simple matter to divert the printers detailed to the contractors by the Army, cut off the subsidies, take back the equipment lent to the contractors—and the contractors would have had to surrender to any terms the Secretary might offer them. He could then keep those he needed, get rid of those who were inefficient, quarrelsome or unnecessary and make sure that all the printing work done benefitted the Treasury alone so that it would be able to meet its needs. It says something about the desperate straits in which he found himself that Memminger overcame his prejudices on the point to at least make inquiries as to its feasibility.

The reply that he got from Pope was not very encouraging, certainly not in every particular. As Pope put it in his August 18, 1862 letter:[2]

> I do not think we will mend the matter a great deal by putting three of four contractors in one house and calling them a Government establishment. They would quarrel still, and perhaps worse than ever. All want to be masters, and all want the profits . This is the whole truth, and all the trouble they have been giving me had been in their efforts to outdo each other. All wish to dictate

> just as soon as you do not yield to their particular schemes...
>
> In fact, if it was not that I feel that I would not be doing my duty to my country, I would kick them all over together and quit. I have never been so annoyed in my life. They deliberately desire to use me to outwit each other. It is impossible for you at a distance to see the will and won't policy of these contractors...These contractors have no idea of doing anything that will take away from the profits. To counteract all of this, I would with great deference propose that a real Government establishment be inaugurated (for a long time after a peace these notes will have to be used), and to this end I have suggested that paper in large quantity be imported, and lithographic material, as well as steel-plate material and presses, and men in sufficient quantities to put the Government beyond the control of contractors.

The Secretary, perhaps because of his confidence in the capabilities of Pope and no doubt governed by his desire to avoid a Government currency after the war (which the absence of a Government establishment would neatly impede), chose not to act on this advice, although he did promulgate various rules at Pope's suggestion, which greatly limited the scope of the printers' powers, cut off the magpie-like stealing of one another's personnel and some of their other shoddy practices.

There only remained the question of what to do about the currency. For manifestly, as the counterfeiting panic had proved, there was no way in which they could continue along the disastrous course already pursued. The currency needed to be standardized, and improved in quality and measures taken to speed up its production by cutting out as much individual plate-making as possible. Once again, Memminger turned to Pope and an extensive study was made of the whole subject. And since the views of the contractors, with the exception of Keatinge on purely technical matters, was hardly disinterested, Pope leaned heavily on the views of George Dunn, the leader of the Scottish lithographers, who was destined to become a small-time contractor in Richmond during 1863-65.

As George Dunn summarized his views, which were passed on to Secretary Memminger:[3]

> Sir: Supplementary to the short conversation I had with you on Thursday last, in which I briefly pointed out the necessity for adopting a different course than hitherto

pursued with the engraved issues of Confederate paper, I beg to state that, having examined the issues, in no instance is there an original design, either in denominational ornament or vignette, to be found in one of these notes. The centralization of bank-note engraving as a system, and the very fine style in which American paper has been gotten up in New York, are points long since acknowledged. Machinery may be found there not more to be admired for construction than admirably adapted for producing any kind of device requisite to fine variety and beauty to promissory notes. The engraving of the figures and vignettes has reached a point approximating perfection; but the very limited number of first-class draughtsmen and engravers, compared with the enormous demand for paper in America, arising out of its low denominational value, has given rise to an injudicious use of the transfer press for reproducing engravings on both steel and copper. In this and other ways, demand has been met, and the first great element of security for a note, viz., originality of design in the ornament as in the writing, has been lost sight of. Any artist contented with excellence and beauty only, and satisfied to ignore invention altogether in his productions, may find all the assistance he requires in any of the many aids to engravers published in the North; but the duplicate engraved plates being also there, he is very much at the mercy of the men whose ideas he borrows.

Practical men in England had some difficulty in deciding how you would overcome those connected with your circulation, New York being the producing place; they had no idea you would adopt a plan of operation which gives to the men in the North the power to issue the originals you have been content to copy. There has been exhibited a want of prudent thought on this subject most culpable; and as Government officials could hardly be expected to be acquainted with all the minutiae of the art, the enormous injury inflicted on the Confederacy is fairly to be charged against those who have set up this system of imitation. Three designs for dollar bills were shown to me last week about to be forwarded to Colonel Memminger for his approval by Mr. Keatinge. If this gentleman did not perceive the danger in which he stood as to professional reputation, he might at least have discovered how much he jeopardized the Confederate States circulation. Bills got up in the style of these is just imitation "made easy." Profusely and elaborately ornamented as they were, they showed some perfect gems of art, but the condemning fact was just as palpable as their beauty. Without one redeeming exception, every item of ornament was a specimen from an existing engraving. If we cannot altogether defy spurious issues, we need not assist them. If we cannot, for present want of machinery and material, come up to that degree of excellence which has been attained in the North, let us adopt a style of our own, and for the perfections of a lengthened experience substitute originality of idea. I do not enter on the question of printing from engraved plates transferred to stone, or from the plates themselves, or to the question of electrotypic art as used in the Bank of England for note production. To accomplish the Government intentions, except by printing from engraved plates transferred to stone, at least from 150 to 200 copper-plate presses would be required. This fact for the present establishes lithography as a necessity....

Certain points made in Dunn's letter require commentary and amplification.

First, there can be very little doubt as to the lack of originality of the Confederate currency up to that time. With the exception of the Confederate leaders' portraits appearing on such notes, there was nothing new in the whole series. It was not merely that the lettering and vignettes were copied from notes already in circulation in the South, the originals being, as Dunn properly pointed out, in the North; it was no less true that whole notes or parts of them had been copied from plates available in the South, the masters of which were also in the North. For example, The first Leggett, Keatinge & Ball notes, types 23 and 32[4] were reengravings of the notes of the Farmers and Mechanics Bank of Savannah; the green portion of the type 21 note was taken from a plate for the Commercial Bank of Columbus, Mississippi. Likewise, as has been demonstrated in the March 1972 edition of *The Numismatist*,[5] the Indian Princess note, the Women with urn-Eagle and Shield notes (types 35, 27, 28) were all created from plates lent by the Bank of Charleston, South Carolina. And the spoils of the American Bank Note Company branch in New Orleans yielded the plates of the *Banque des Ameliorations* of New Orleans, which in turn was converted for use on the Keatinge and Ball types 33 and 34 $5 bills. Still worse, much of this art work was 20 years or more behind the times, had lost its copyright protection, and was no longer to be had just at American Bank Note. Anyone so minded could become an accomplished counterfeiter with just that ease cited by Dunn.

But having diagnosed the evil, what was to be done? There was neither time nor money to import the men and material to emulate European bank note printing nor, given the southern conservatism, would public opinion have looked with favor upon so radical a departure from past practice. The solution was to keep the general appearance of American notes while doing work that was as original as possible. Obviously, there was not time to redo everything, but much of what had been done did have some distinct features and those should and could be exploited. Accordingly, notice was sent to all the engravers of the government's intention to create a uniform type note for each denomination and for those interested to submit to a committee appointed by the Secretary their proposals as to how the new notes ought to look. Therefore, Keatinge in July 1862 came to Richmond to make drawings of Confederate leaders, soldiers, buildings and so forth in order to furnish new designs for the upcoming contest. On September 6, the Committee met and after reviewing the various proposed signs forwarded a report with their recommendations to Secretary Memminger, as follows:[6]

> Sir: In obedience to your instructions, we beg leave to report that designs for Confederate notes have been submitted to us by Colonel Duncan, Messrs. Keatinge & Ball, George Dunn, and Messrs. Paterson & Co. To save time and have the aid of some experience, we invited Messrs. William Thayer, of the Bank of Charleston; E. J. Scott, of the Commercial Bank of Columbia; and Mr. Strobel, of the Farmers' and Exchange Bank of Charleston, to meet with us and examine the designs. Assisted by them, we have made the following selections: One dollar note, with the head of Mr. Yancey, of Alabama, designed by Messrs. Keatinge & Ball, has been selected without alteration.
>
> Two dollar note, with the head of Mr. Benjamin, Secretary of State, designed by Messrs. Keatinge & Ball, has been selected without alteration.
>
> Five-dollar note, with the head of the Secretary of the Treasury (as appears in Mr. Dunn's design), has been composed from designs furnished by Messrs. Keatinge & Ball and Mr. Dunn, as follows: The lettering of the note as designed by Mr. Dunn; the medallion with the figure "5" to be put on the upper corner over the head of the

Secretary of the Treasury; on the left end of the note heavy machine-work of the pattern of that exhibited upon the note of Keatinge & Ball to be extended to the top of the note, with the word "five" printed as in the 1's, 2's, and 5's of Messrs. Keatinge & Ball; with a view of the Capitol at Richmond, enlarged, from the drawing of Mr. Dunn, as a centre vignette.

Ten-dollar note, with the head of Mr. Hunter, of Virginia, and Capitol of South Carolina, as designed by Mr. Dunn. In fact we take Mr. Dunn's design, with the following alterations: One of the medallion "X's"—a design of Messrs. Keatinge & Ball—to be put in the right-hand upper corner, over the head of Mr. Hunter; the machine-work on the left-hand end of the "ten" of Messrs. Keatinge & Ball to be put on the left-hand of the ten selected, with the word "ten" printed as in the "ten note" of Messrs. Keatinge & Ball. The likeness of Mr. Hunter, as in Mr. Dunn's note, to be preserved.

Twenty-dollar note, with the head of Mr. Stephens, the Vice-President, in lower right-hand corner, without scroll; one of the "XX medallions" to be put in the upper right-hand corner (without the scroll), over the head of Mr. Stephens; the left-hand end of the note to be ornamented with machine-work of the pattern now in the lower left-hand corner, to be extended to the top word "twenty," printed as in the other notes of Messrs. Keatinge & Ball, with a view of the State-House at Nashville, as represented by the drawing of Mr. Dunn (for a centre vignette), to be enlarged to suit the space allowed in design of Messrs. Keatinge & Ball.

The details of the notes to be left to Mr. Keatinge, according to the instructions of the Secretary of the Treasury.

The machine-work for the back of the notes is to be left also to Mr. Keatinge, with the understanding that he is to get up a different back for each denominational words "One Dollar," "Two Dollars," "Five Dollars," &c., printed twice, in letters of proper size, so as to cross each other on the back of the note.

From the difficulty of obtaining coloring matter, so as to have all the notes alike, we would recommend that the back of the 1's and 2's be printed in red; the back of the 5's, 10's, and 20's (circulating bills) in green; the interest 100's now used to have the "hundred" on the face left out, and the back in green, with the words "interest hundred" printed straight across the back from left to right; the circulating 50's and 100's to have the words "fifty dollars" and "hundred dollars" straight across the back.

We would further report, without going into details now, that we consider it perfectly practicable to make transfers in the Government establishment, and that Mr. McGown, with a part or the whole of the force now on the Government supply, will be able to furnish the tranfers necessary to all the lithographic establishments.

Very respectfully, JOS. DANIEL POPE.
S. G. JAMISON.

Here too, some commentary and explanation is clearly necessary as the designs proposed and forwarded to the Secretary both as regards the face and the backs were significantly altered, if not completely discarded before the notes reached the form as issued. An important point is that the $1 note used a portrait of Senator Clement C. Clay of Alabama, rather than Senator Yancy. This substitution was politically, not artistically motivated. Yancy had become an opponent of President Davis and Secretary Memminger was not about to honor a man on the outs with his chief. While there is no correspondence to confirm this interpretation, the effort to change the design of the $100 note in November 1862, after Secretary of War Randolph had resigned in a huff because of what he felt was excessive Presidential meddling in the affairs of his Department, together with a failure to consult before decisions were made, allows us to infer such a substitution. For,on that occasion, Memminger hurriedly wrote asking for the design to be changed, but as the only suitable substitute from a size standpoint was a portrait of Patrick Henry, which was available in the North, the decision was made to stick to the original vignette and the situation had to be explained to the President. Evidently Davis did not insist on a change, and Randolph was thus honored even after his abrupt resignation.

Another key point was in the matter of the back tints. The proposed design for the $1, $2 and $5 notes to be printed in red, was discarded, the back of the $5 note was printed in blue, as was originally planned only for the $20 and the $10 bills. The lower denomination notes in fact received no backs at all. The reason for this change was twofold. First, there was not enough ink available and second, another printing, with its attendant delays was not desired. Moreover, the Government had discovered that they could have pink paper manufactured in the South which would provide the color without the time delays that a second printing entailed.

Quite clearly, despite the competition of others, there were only two engravers in the Confederacy capable of doing work up to the standard expected by the committee and of the two (Keatinge and Dunn), to judge by the work of each that was accepted, Keatinge was clearly the superior. It is true that the Treasury had to make do with lithography, rather than engraved work, but a comparison of the early $20 bills done by the Scottish lithographers with the engraving work done by Keatinge shows such a high quality level of reproduction that the difference was not sufficient to justify the extra work and ink in doing this work the more elaborate way. Indeed, Secretary Memminger for a long time thought that the backs of the $100 and $50 notes were engraved, whereas, with the exeption of the earlier issues and those made from leftover plates, all are lithographs.

This improvement in quality coupled with speedier methods of production cut off counterfeiting on any serious basis until the end of the war and allowed the Government to meet its bills more effectively for another year. Then, confronted with a demand beyond their productive capacity coupled with the demands imposed upon them by a massive new funding program, the system broke down and the Treasury fell hopelessly behind. The fault for this lay more with a Congress which failed to impose taxes to check the inflation than with the printers. And if the printers were not as successful as might have been desired, they still did quite well vis-à-vis the North with all its resources, which itself was often a month in arrears on its obligations.

1 Raphael P. Thian, ed., *Correspondence with the Treasury Department of the Confederate States of America, 1861-1865, Appendix*, Part 5, 1861-62 (Washington, 1884), pp. 588-89.

2 Pope to Memminger, August 18, 1862, in Thian, *Correspondence*, pp. 596-98.

3 Dunn to Pope, August 19, 1862, in Thian, *Correspondence*, pp. 599-601.

4 Type references are to Grover C. Criswell, *Confederate and Southern States Currency*, 2nd ed. (Citra, FL, 1976).

5 Douglas B. Ball, "Confederate Currency Derived from Banknote Plates," *The Numismatist* 1972, pp. 339-52.

The CSA Bank Convention of 1861 and Its Delegates

Carl W.A. Carlson

Coinage of the Americas Conference
at The American Numismatic Society, New York

Two great economic truths were swiftly recognized in the South following Secession: first, the newly formed central government could not function, much less wage war, without money; and second, the chartering of banks under different codes within the various southern states made necessary some sort of voluntary system under which they could work together across state lines in support of national and regional economic requirements. Accordingly, urged on by the Tennessee Legislature, and doubtless encouraged by the new central government in Richmond, some of the major southern banks sent delegates to an initial Bank Convention in Atlanta at the beginning of June 1861. Resolutions were passed by that Convention on June 3, 1861, recommending that all southern banks receive and pay out Treasury notes of the CSA government; that they advance the government money against deposit of high denomination Treasury notes or stocks and bonds; that the railroad companies be urged to accept Treasury notes for fares and freight bills; that the legislatures of the various states pass measures to allow Treasury notes to be used for the payment of taxes; and a variety of related measures. The Convention, headed by Gazaway Bugg Lamar of Savannah, Georgia, then adjourned to meet again on July 24 in Richmond.

The Convention reassembled on the appointed date with a substantial increase both in the number of delegates attending and in the number of banks represented; Lamar was again in the Chair. This second meeting of the Bank Convention lasted through July 26 and produced numerous resolutions reinforcing those of the earlier meeting and adding further details to the suggestions made at that time. Following opening services and the reading of the minutes of the previous meeting, President Lamar informed the delegates that he had been in contact with Memminger, Secretary of the Treasury of the CSA, and had learned from him that, during the adjournment of the Convention in June and July, Memminger had received letters from various CSA banks agreeing in general with the proposals initially set forth.

The Convention then acted swiftly on a series of motions and resolutions: hearty approval of the government's action in prosecuting the war against the United States; general agreement that southern resources were more than adequate to handle a war, and that the delegates to the Convention would contribute their aid to render those resources available to the public; that it was the duty of banks, capitalists, and property holders to provide monetary and other support to the central government during the war; and that a committee of one delegate per state be set up to receive and present resolutions to the Convention as a whole. Having passed these resolutions, the Convention adjourned until July 25.

By the time of the next meeting on July 25, further delegates had arrived; these were duly introduced to the Convention and took their seats. Ramsey, President of the Bank of Tennessee branch at Knoxville, then moved to invite Secretary Memminger to participate in the Convention; this resolution passed promptly and a delegation was selected to present the invitation. Two major motions were passed on to the Committee on Business: one, that banks would receive and pay out the notes of all other banks in the CSA during the war, as designated by the banks then represented in the Convention from those states then represented; and the other the establishment of a committee to explore the expediency of, and necessary measures for, engraving and printing bank notes and manufacturing bank note paper within the CSA.

By the time these measures had been dealt with, the delegation reported back that it had extended the Convention's invitation to Secretary Memminger and that he was then present in the hall. Upon being presented to the Convention by President Lamar, Memminger thanked the delegates for their support of the government and offered some suggestions for their consideration. Following Memminger's talk, the Convention considered a series of other resolutions which, after discussion, were referred to committee: one proposed that, since many farmers and planters had voluntarily subscribed a portion of their forthcoming crops of cotton and other produce to aid the government, the banks should advance such farmers and planters the sums they might need prior to harvest, such loans to be repaid to the banks when the crops were sold; another proposed that all banks in the CSA would receive and pay out each other's notes and also all CSA notes from $5 to $100, the balances due between banks to be settled in CSA notes; and a third recommending that banks agreeing to the proposals of the Convention should limit the circulation of their own notes so as not to exceed their actual capital.

On the recommendation of Secretary Memminger, the Committee on Business was asked to consider, and report to the Convention upon, the nature of post notes which they felt it would be advisable for the Government to issue; what amount of such notes might safely be placed in circulation; and whether or not it would seem advisable to control, through advances on produce, the crops of cotton and other non-perishables in case the Union blockade was maintained. Another of the delegates then proposed a resolution to the effect that the Convention recommended the issue of Treasury notes, most of which should bear 5 percent interest per year; and further, as a separate resolution, that any attempt by the Convention at that date to interfere with existing regulations on the receiving and paying out of notes, with the exception of the agreement to handle the Treasury notes, would be highly inadvisable. This latter point was basically a States' Rights platform introduced into a Convention whose very meeting proclaimed the necessity of central operations extending across state boundaries if the Confederacy were to be able to carry on the war successfully. It was to return to haunt them very shortly.

This rapid growth in the number of matters referred to the Committee on Business led to a motion to increase the number of members of that committee so that it might be able to complete its tasks within some reasonable time period; this passed, and the President added seven more members to it. The Convention then adjourned for the day.

When the Convention reopened on the morning of July 26, a lengthy series of resolutions was proposed to deal with one of the most difficult problems facing the Convention members: the constitutional prohibition in the State of Louisiana against suspension of specie payments and the issuance of paper notes instead, which was basically what was being proposed as general policy for the delegate banks in accepting and paying out the proposed CSA Treasury notes. The resolutions proposed urged that the Louisiana banks take steps as rapidly as possible to assemble, if necessary, a state convention to nullify or revoke the constitutional provision in question; that they press for this vigorously; that the Governor of Louisiana be requested to cooperate in the matter; and that the Secretary of the Convention should forward the entire proceedings of the Bank Convention to the Louisiana Governor and to all the Louisiana banks. At the request of the proposer, these resolutions were tabled temporarily.

The Standing Committee then proposed that all banks in the CSA should make arrangements with the major banks in the cities to receive notes of those banks in payment and on deposit, and that those banks so doing should post public notice of their arrangements so that soldiers would not be subjected to discounts on their pay through dealing with banks which were not parties to such arrangements. This was adopted. The Committee also recommended acceptance of the earlier motion for the banks to make advances to planters who had pledged part of their future crops to the aid of the government, but that other proposals regarding control of crops be postponed until a later meeting of the Convention when the situation might have stabilized or changed significantly. This was also accepted. After a few other motions had been handled—most of them being referred to the Committee on Business—the President read a letter from the two delegates from the Crescent City Bank in Louisiana (the only bank in that State which had sent delegates) politely requesting that their names be removed from the list of delegates since they had found out that no other banks from Louisiana were going to be represented at the Convention and thus felt themselves in a rather awkward position. The Convention then adjourned until late afternoon.

The evening session on July 26 marked the conclusion of this second meeting of the Bank Convention. It was largely occupied with the presentation of the recommendations of the Committee on Business. These recommendations, embodied in a formal report, included the opinion that it would be safe for the CSA Government to issue "at least one hundred millions of dollars, in addition to the notes already authorized by law"[1] as the members of the Committee felt certain that such notes would be willingly accepted by the citizens and the banks and would soon become the currency of the country. A further resolution they proposed modified one made earlier at the first Convention by stating that banks represented at this session of the Convention would receive and pay out such Treasury notes as "may be issued by the Government," thus accepting in advance all future note issues. They also urged all banks which were not represented at the Convention to adopt a similar resolution and send it to Secretary Memminger.

Since it was clearly the intention of the government that these Treasury notes serve the function of a currency system, the committee recommended that all notes of a given issue bear the same date of issue and carry the same rate of interest, to reduce confusion and difficulty on the part of tellers and others in handling them and calculating the interest due on the individual notes. They recommended an interest rate of 2 cents per day per $100, which worked out to 7.3 percent per annum; that the notes be redeemable in three years or less, at the option of the government, and that they be convertible at the choice of the holder into 8 percent stocks or bonds; also, that they be receivable for all public dues except the cotton export tax. They also recommended that notes from $5 to $20 should not bear interest as they would function as the basic notes within the currency system.

A few other items remained to be handled after acceptance of the committee's report: a delegation was sent to President Davis to see when he might be able to meet the delegates briefly; assorted standing committees were composed to prepare for a future meeting of the Convention in October; James Rose of South Carolina succeeded Lamar as President; and a final resolution of importance to bank and Treasury note students was passed, calling the attention of enterprising persons to the need for an establishment in the CSA to produce bank note paper and engraving plates and for actually producing the needed notes. With notice from the delegation that CSA President Davis would receive the Convention delegates at 9 o'clock that evening, the Bank Convention adjourned. It had accomplished perhaps more than it had expected, but many problems remained, the majority of them having to do with the States' Rights factor—especially in Louisiana and western Alabama—and the complications of the Union blockade and eventual staggering inflation.

Perhaps the most important factor left unresolved was the Louisiana situation: since Louisiana banks were forbidden to suspend specie payments and use paper notes instead, they could not cooperate in the general bank resolve across the South to receive and pay out the CSA Treasury notes. The matter was further complicated by the close connections between Louisiana finances and those of southern and western Alabama, including Mobile; if the Louisiana banks had to operate on a specie basis, then so did the nearby Alabama banks for the practical reason of staying in business. Since specie was virtually unobtainable in quantity anywhere in the South after 1861, handling of payment for any government project was very difficult. In the long run, the inability of the banks and the Government to make payments in specie in Louisiana and adjacent areas meant that work on the vital ironclad gunboats being built in New Orleans was slowed by the difficulty of obtaining parts and also by massive labor disputes. Those gunboats were still incomplete when the Union fleet attacked up the Mississippi and captured New Orleans (which they would have had great difficulty doing if the boats had been ready for their approach). The loss of New Orleans and control of the lower Mississippi eventually cost the South the war, so we may say with justification that the situation that led the Louisiana delegates to withdraw from the Richmond Convention was ultimately a contributing cause of the defeat of the CSA itself.

A complete list of the delegates to the Bank Convention in Richmond has survived; and is included at the end of this article. Altogether, 51 banks from 7 states (including, initially, Louisiana) were represented, most of them sending the President of the bank. Some sent two representatives, and five of the banks sent three delegates. The smallest delegations included Louisiana (two delegates from a single bank) and Alabama (three delegates representing the

Central Bank); in both cases the Louisiana specie problem was involved, as discussed earlier. The other states involved were Georgia, North Carolina, South Carolina, Tennessee, and Virginia (which, of course, was hosting the meeting). Had anything (such as a Union raid in strength) happened to the Convention, the Southern banking community would have been decimated at its highest levels.

We know some details concerning a few of these delegates. For example, the Cashier of the Planters and Mechanics Bank in South Carolina was Clement Hoffman Stevens, born in Norwich, Connecticut, in 1821. At the start of the Civil War he was placed in charge of building the fortifications and armored battery on Morris Island; in 1862 he was commissioned Colonel of the 24th South Carolina Infantry Regiment, and was promoted to Brigadier General in 1864. At the end of July of that year, he was killed in the battle of Peach Tree Creek during the Atlanta campaign. The President of the Knoxville branch of the Bank of Tennessee was Dr. James Gettys McGready Ramsey, born in Knoxville in 1797 and doubtless one of the major forces in getting the Tennessee Legislature to urge the convening of a banking convention. He practiced medicine in Knoxville from 1820 on, and was a Director of the Louisville, Cincinnati and Charleston Railroad. He was also President of the Knoxville branch of the Southwestern Railroad Bank (whose President, James Rose, succeeded Lamar as head of the Bank Convention). Ramsey served as President of the Tennessee Historical Society from 1874 until 1884; he died in Knoxville in April of that year.

We have seen something of Lamar's role as President of the Bank Convention during its first two meetings in Atlanta and Richmond. In addition to serving as President, he represented two Georgia banks: the Bank of Commerce, Savannah, of which he was President, and the Bank of Columbus; he also had a financial interest in

the Mechanics Bank of Augusta, of which his brother was Cashier. He was born in Georgia in 1798. In 1834 he built the steamer John Randolph, the first iron steamboat in American waters, and was a founder in the next year of the Iron Steamboat Company of Augusta, Georgia, operating on the Savannah River. From 1845 until 1861, he was President of the Bank of the Republic in New York City, and he represented CSA interests there as agent during 1860-61, purchasing and shipping south large amounts of arms and ammunition and becoming involved in the attempt to have bank note plates engraved in New York City for the CSA. During the Civil War he served as head of blockade running operations for the CSA; when the famous Stonewall Jackson memorial medals, which had been made in Europe, were run through the blockade in 1864 and reached Savannah, it was in one of Lamar's warehouses that they were buried to keep the Union forces from finding them.

These three interesting characters, who were delegates to the Bank Convention in Richmond, were also signers of bank notes for their own banks in their regular capacity within those organizations. We currently know, from actual observation, of 38 delegates who signed circulating notes from 37 represented banks, and there are probably others on the list of whom we have not yet seen a signed note. We have seen one of the interconnections between delegates in the case of Ramsey and Rose. We also have some reason to believe that Lamar (running the steamboat line on the Savannah River as well as the Bank of Commerce) was connected by marriage with James Rose of the Southwestern Railroad Bank in South Carolina, and that both of these men were connected with J.W. Davies of the Georgia Railroad and Banking Company by marriage, thus establishing a river and rail network covering much of the South and handling a very profitable volume of goods. Doubtless there were similar connections between others of the major financial figures in the relatively small and compact southern banking community. We also, as it happens, know the name of Lamar's opposite number in 1861, the man who served as Chairman of the banker's commission which agreed to cover the first Federal War Loan: Moses Taylor, President of the City Bank in NYC from 1855 on, Controller of the Delaware, Lackawanna and Western Railroad from 1857 on, Treasurer of the first Atlantic cable venture, President of the Lackawanna Coal and Iron Company, and later Treasurer of the Marquette, Houghton and Ontonagon Railroad in Michigan.

Members of the southern banking community cease to be just signatures on obsolete notes when we can observe tham at work in other areas, and serving as delegates to the 1861 Convention. We can begin to realize what a small group of men were in charge of the major share of the wealth of the South, and how vital their cooperation was to the new CSA government; from their roles in the Convention, and the resolutions they proposed and passed, we can see how vitally interested they were in the success of that new government. It all adds a new dimension to obsolete note collecting, and an increased pleasure.

Delegates to the Southern Bank Convention of 1861

ALABAMA

Central Bank of Alabama: *Wm. Knox* (Pres.),[2] Chas. T. Pollard, J. Whiting.

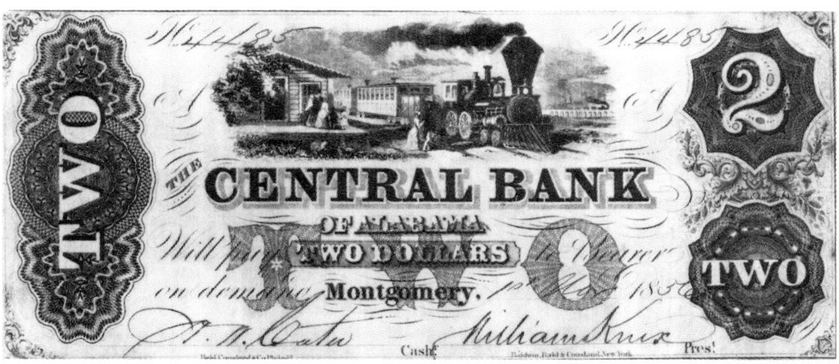

GEORGIA

Bank of Commerce, Savannah: *G.B. Lamar* (Pres.).
Bank of Columbus: G.B. Lamar.
Bank of Middle Georgia: W.B. Johnston.
Merchants and Mechanics Bank, Macon: *W.B. Johnston*.
Planters Bank of the State: *R.R. Cuyler*.
Central RR and Banking Co. of Georgia: R.R. Cuyler.
Mechanics Bank of Augusta: *Thos. S. Metcalf* (Pres.).
City Bank, Augusta: Thos. Barrett.
Geeorgia RR and Banking Co.: J.W. Davies.

LOUISIANA

Crescent City Bank: W.C. Tompkins, J.O. Nixon.

NORTH CAROLINA

Bank of the State of N.C.: *G.W. Mordecai.*
Bank of Cape Fear: W.A. Wright.
Farmers Bank of N.C.: *W.A. Caldwell* (Cash.).
Bank of Yanceyville: *Thos. D. Johnston* (Pres., earlier Cash.).
Bank of Clarendon: *John D. Williams* (Pres.).
Commercial Bank of Wilmington: *O.G. Parsley* (Pres.).
Bank of Washington: *James E. Hoyt* (Pres.).
Miners & Planters Bank: *A.T. Davidson* (Pres.).
Bank of Fayetteville: *W.G. Broadfoot* (Pres., earlier Cash.).
Bank of Lexington: *B.A. Kittrell* (Pres.).
Bank of Lexington, Graham Branch: E.F. Watson.
Bank of Wadesborough: *H.B. Hammond* (Pres., earlier Cash.).

SOUTH CAROLINA

Bank of the State of S.C.: *C.M. Furman*, C.V. Chamberlain (Pres.).
Bank of South Carolina: *George B. Reid* (Pres., earlier Cash.).

State Bank: Wm. C. Bee, Robert Mure, G.M. Coffin.
Union Bank of S.C.: *W.B. Smith* (Pres.).
Planters & Mechanics Bank: J.J. McCarter, *C.H. Stevens*(Cash.), C.T. Mitchell
Bank of Charleston: *J.K. Sass* (Pres.), George A. Trenholm.
Southwestern RR Bank: *James Rose* (Pres.), J.G. Holmes.
Farmers & Exchange Bank: *John S. Davies* (Pres.).
Peoples Bank: *D.L. McKay*, Jos. S. Gibbs (Pres.).
Merchants Bank of S.C. at Cheraw: Allan McFarlan.
Bank of Georgetown: *J.G. Henning* (Pres.).
Bank of Chester: *George S. Cameron* (Pres.).
Exchange Bank: John Caldwell.
Bank of Hamburg: *J.W. Stokes* (Pres.), Wm. Gregg.

TENNESSEE

Bank of Tennessee: *G.C. Torbett.*
Bank of Tennessee, Memphis Branch: Jos. Lenow.
Bank of Tennessee, Knoxville Branch: *J.G.M. Ramsey* (Pres.).
Bank of West Tennessee: *T.A. Nelson* (Pres.).
Bank of Memphis: M.J. Wicks.
Planters Bank, Memphis Branch: D.A. Shepherd.

VIRGINIA

Farmers Bank of Virginia: *W.H. Macfarlane* (Pres.).
Bank of Virginia: *James Caskie* (Pres.), A.T. Harris, J.L. Bacon.
Exchange Bank: L.W. Glazebrook, W.P. Strother.
Bank of the Commonwealth: *L. Nunnally (Pres.), J.B. Morton*, J.A. Jones.

Merchants Bank of Virginia: *C.R. Slaughter* (Pres.).
The Danville Bank: *W.T. Sutherlin* (Pres.).
Bank of Richmond: *Alexander Warwick* (Pres.).
Traders Bank of Richmond: *A. Johnson*, Hector Davis, E. Denton.

[1] The Proceedings of the Richmond Convention are published, most conveniently, in "Proceedings of the Bank Convention of the Confederate States," *The Essay-Proof Journal* 102 (1969), pp. 76-83, with illustration of the original title page on p. 76.

[2] Delegates who signed issued notes are indicated in italics.

An Historian's View of the State Bank Notes: A Mirror of Life in the Early Republic

Elvira Clain-Stefanelli

Coinage of the Americas Conference
at The American Numismatic Society, New York

It is an auspicious opportunity when we come in direct contact with contemporary artifacts; in our instance, numismatic items serve as such first hand documents, defeating the contention of many historians that numismatics is not easily approachable by the historic researcher. Coins and money in general can be an excellent inspiration to the historian, they being after all the *nervus rerum gerendarum*, the means which put in motion the entire life of the past: its politics; its wars; its riches; its arts. But in order to reach valid historical conclusions, we need to subject coins to a complex research program. In our case the state and private bank notes which were produced during the first half of the nineteenth century speak in good part for themselves. A kaleidoscope mirroring the entire spectrum of people's lives, activities and feelings unfolds in an unbelievable richness and never-ending succession of miniature paintings.

It has happened to me only twice in my numismatic career that I have been astounded by a numismatic history book illustrated by the very people of that period: one is the series of Roman Republican denarii, depicting in hundreds of coin images the mythology and history of that remote period, and then again the stupendous series of vignettes which embellish the so-called ''obsolete'' notes of the United States. Departing from the very official, rigid and terse emblematic appearance of currency notes in general, bankers of that period entered into a frenzied competition to outdo each other by rendering their notes varied, attractive and meaningful.

There might have been a similarity between the moneyers of the Roman Republic and the bankers of the early United States: both were avidly seeking to capture the interest of the public. The Roman moneyers tried to further their political careers—their *cursus honorum*—the U.S. bankers attempted to gain the support of the public at large in order to increase their business. I am tempted to ascribe to these ambitions the basic incentive to create a medium of circulation which varied drastically from the general aspect of currency. The Roman moneyers had to extoll the deeds of their ancestors, which could not be shown only by a symbolic figure but required a representation of a more complex scene. The American bankers produced a similar storybook on their currencies. They were the creators of a capital which was at the base of the growth of the new country. Banking was a free enterprise and bankers were therefore in fierce competition with each other. It is interesting to remark that the Roman Republican denarii were created in a period of intense growth as were the state and private U.S. bank notes. It was the period of the introduction of mechanization, of the locomotive, of the steamship, of budding industrialization, and, at the same time, of the development of the backbone of the national economy—farming and cattle-raising. People worked hard to tame the new lands and transform them into a rich productive country. It was, in a different form, the *El Dorado* of which settlers of the western world had dreamed so often. People were conscious and proud of their achievements, and nobody was more so than the banker who was at the root of all these achievements. He wanted the world to know what the people had created, and at the same time, entice them to do more. Why design posters or write brochures telling about your accomplishments when you can put little "posters," illustrated with the most varied scenes, into the hands of everybody? It was one of the most ingenious advertising machines ever envisioned.

These were the psychological motives to create this most unusual kind of currency. In addition, bankers could count on a tradition of art appreciation in the country. From studies of the seventeenth century engravings and wood-cuts in the Colonies, we gain the impression that homes were often decorated with various prints, as a traveler remarked in Williamsburg "that I almost fancied myself in...some...elegant print shop."[1] The description of prints of the eighteenth century indicate a great variety of subjects—nature and city views, Indian portraits together with so-called "heads," authentic and imaginary portraits of contemporaries. The public was used to seeing prints even with a classical and historical content, collect them and hang them in their homes. Therefore to see their money decorated with similar engravings would not seem unusual to them.

As to the artistic value of these vignettes, we know who created them; the printing companies seldom failed to put their names in fairly visible locations on these notes. There is a long roster of names of printing firms, ending with the exceptionally active American Bank Note Company. We even know in some instances the engravers of the vignettes, but we ought to know more about the source of inspiration of those artists—an enormously vast and complicated research field. I tried to cut the Gordian knot by asking myself about the motive in selecting certain themes or subjects. We know that special sample books were prepared by the printing companies which facilitated the choice of the bankers. I see in their preference for particular themes the key to the mentality which dominated not only the business world of those decades but which also reflected, to a certain extent, the way of thinking and feeling of an entire nation.

My point of departure in examining these design elements is the assumption that no matter what the personal tastes or motives of the bankers were, they would not have continued to impose a selection and a style which would have been displeasing to the majority of their customers. Sinclair Hitchings stated in an article on the graphic arts in colonial New England that: "The graphic art... produced in New England in the seventeenth century was the result of what people in the colonies needed, what they had time for, and that for which they were willing to spend money."[2] I am certain that not everybody felt the same way about the selection of themes or of their rendition, but the large majority must have enjoyed it; otherwise the richly illustrated currencies could not have survived for half a century.

As an historian I have always been interested in the way people thought or felt during the various periods of history. We know from our own experience how much the mentality of our own pre- and postwar generations varied, and how difficult it is for them to understand each other. Therefore, I find it invaluable to discover a window which permits us to look directly into the way of thinking of generations removed by more than 100 years from our own world. Of course any historian has to ask how authentic, how true to real life are these myriad pictures? The answer cannot be straightforward; it has to be subjected to rigorous scrutiny in each case. But as a general introductory statement I feel safe in asserting that they render a true picture of the artistic taste of the period. As to the inspiration for many vignettes, I am touching again upon a large undisclosed chapter which could reveal fascinating aspects. Art and art objects were not unknown to the American public in the early 1800s. Some of the famous collectors and artists who traveled and studied abroad were perfectly informed about the great art trends in Europe, which certainly have served as inspiration to many engravers, disseminating this aristocratic hobby among the masses. I would like to accentuate only the fact that special attention should be paid also to the various ethnic groups in the country who might have favored their native art or artists.

Whoever is familiar with the *genre* paintings of the past century will feel immediately at home with the style of most of the vignettes. We are at the end of the Romantic and Biedermeier period when artists shied away from the harshness of reality, and enveloped everything in a hue of eternal beatitude. The bucolic happiness which some vignettes exude should not be viewed as an intended distortion of reality, but as an expression of the artistic taste of the period which permeated not only the graphic arts, but also literature and poetry. Therefore, when using the vignettes as illustrations of life in the early 1800s, we should be aware that we are often looking through a rose-colored filter, and search for the reality, which is there and unfolds in an almost neverending variety of aspects.

Many vignettes furnish us with a lot of historically valid information and greatly enrich our understanding of the material culture as well as of life in general in the United States 150 years ago. I am afraid that this paper instead of answering questions will actually map out a rather long series of new aspects.

I intend only to sketch out some of the main aspects or categories which I have extracted from the great multitude of subjects. These include: early settlers and historical scenes; the ethnic environment—the Indian and the Black; family life; farming; transportation—trains, ships, bridges, canals; occupations; city views; buildings; monuments; and, not to be overlooked, an endless number of male and female portraits; allegories; mythological scenes, and even saints. There are indeed only a few aspects of human life which have not been touched upon, such as music, sports and religion. Should these omissions induce us to draw some historical conclusions?

Undoubtedly farming and the inventions of the century, the steam engines, dominate uncontested as the main factors in the economy of the time. It should be noted that the subjects of the vignettes are not necessarily tied to the general characteristics of the areas where they were issued, although often there is a logical connection between the place of issue, the name of the bank and the subject of the vignette—cottonpickers are not easily found in New England, neither is whaling in Kentucky. Therefore we can state, within certain limitations, that the vignettes tended to underscore local patriotism and pride.

Interestingly, the number of vignettes referring to historical events is relatively limited, concentrated mostly on the colonization period and the Revolutionary War: Washington's crossing of the Delaware in the cold December of 1776, after a painting by Thomas Sully; the surrender of Cornwallis at Yorktown, October 1781, after a painting by John Francis Renault;[3] Colonel Marion, the "Swamp Fox" inviting a British officer to share his potato and water dinner, after a painting by John B. White;[4] and the widely used "Signing of the Declaration of Independence," after John Trumbull's famous painting (fig. 1).[5]

The patriotic feeling of the country found strong expression in the countless portraits of political figures, George Washington being overwhelmingly acknowledged as the "founder," the "Father of the Country." Examples include the copy after Gilbert Stuart's

1

2

"Washington on Dorchester Heights,"[6] and another vignette characteristic of Washington's apotheosis, with his bust surrounded by three muses of the arts in semi-classical attire (fig. 2).[7] Benjamin Franklin follows closely as one of the favorite fathers of the country. David Martin's so-called "Thumb Portrait" is an especially well executed art work.[8] From among the hundreds of male portraits of famous or sometimes anonymous national or local personalities, one might note the level of artistic quality in John W. Dodge's portrait of the aging Andrew Jackson,[9] or the likeness of

Major General Thomas Sumter (1734-1832), Revolutionary soldier, copied after an oil of 1795/6 by Rembrandt Peale.[10] Highly interesting is the fact that even famous foreign personalities, such as Napoleon I, or even classical and mythological figures such as Archimedes, Cincinnatus or Atlas found their place on American bank notes. Due somewhat to the public's select knowledge of foreign literature and history, but rather more to ethnic pride are the somewhat primitively designed portraits of German literary figures, such as Johann Wolfgang Goethe[11] and Johann Gottlieb Klopstock, represented by the Northampton Bank in Germanic Pennsylvania of the 1830s.

The female portraits constitute one of the most puzzling chapters in the history of the graphic arts of the American currency. In addition to a few well known figures such as Martha Washington,[12] Dolly Madison, Jenny Lind, and even Josephine Beauharnais, practically dozens of lovely young ladies are represented on paper notes (fig. 3).[13] We cannot escape the impression of romanticized valentine card figures, however incongruous that is in the context of the forbidding dignity of a business document such as a bank note. Many of the lovely ladies must have been the beauty queens of those days or relatives of leading local personalities, who have thus entered anonymously onto the roster of important figures of the early 1800s. Many vignettes do have the pronounced character of an authentic portrait,[14] but to search for their identity is a tremendous job

3

which could be quite rewarding, but must be undertaken with great patience. They all express the general romantic admiration for serenity and aesthetic perfection which permeates practically every scene represented by the artists of those days.

4

5

Family life is idyllic and beautiful; children are well behaved and eager to learn,[15] and life on the farm with all its chores seems leisurely and enjoyable (fig. 4);[16] milkmaids look like fashion models posing in front of a tranquil landscape.[17] No matter how distorted these representations might be, considering the hard life of the farmer and the worker who had to bear the brunt of the tremendous effort to build the country, we cannot dismiss the importance of some vignettes giving us a more realistic picture of the material culture and ambience of the period with their tools and farm utensils. Examples include: a grain cradle;[18] one of the early mechanical reapers, most likely Hussey's reaping machine of the 1830s, not McCormick's famous new invention, since it has a hand rake (fig. 5);[19] one vignette depicts a complex of three agricultural machines—harrow, hay thrower, and another type of mechanized weeder.[20] We are told about the quality of the crops by reference

6

7

to man-high corn; the importance of the cotton industry;[21] haymaking; the making of turpentine (fig.6).[22] Of interest and significance is the attention given to farm animals,[23] such as the horse, sheep, pig, and to scenes dealing with the cattle[24] and meat industry.[25] On one particular note there is even a hog slaughtering scene (fig. 7).[26] Somehow these scenes bring to mind Sandburg and stories of Western "butchers of the world," the cattleman and the sheep rancher.

A country which was rapidly expanding and developing in every way had to show its pride in the industrious people who accomplished the American miracle. Therefore, many occupations are represented on bank notes, from lumberjacks chopping trees,[27] and men loading boards, to masons and stone masons, cobblers[28] and surveyors (fig. 8).[29] The sailor also figures prominently in these notes, generally depicted as a happy young man eager to see the world.[30] Interesting is the representation of two occupations—that of an alchemist[31] and of a drummerboy.

Fascinating are the vignettes depicting one of the most lucrative but most hazardous occupations, that of whaling, which spellbound the world with its haunting stories and lured men far into endless waters. One vignette, "attacking a right whale and cutting in," (fig. 9) is a scene copied after a French marine painter, Louis Garneray (1784-1857).[32] Women are seen not only on the farm, but also in the sweatshops of early industry, as they can be viewed at looms (fig. 10)[33]or yarn-spinning machines.

8

9

10

11

The budding industries were certainly the pride of the country, factories with smoke stacks are not rare on notes,[34] often representing local industries, such as the Franklin Silk Industry in Franklin, Ohio, or symbolizing banks bearing in their titles names such as Manufacturers, or Mechanics. Scenes depicting men working at a forge, in front of glass melting furnaces,[35] or with large machines, can be of great help to industrial historians by giving detailed pictures of tools and of working techniques. Men loading barrels of tobacco point toward another important wealth—the tobacco industry. The mining (mainly coal) industry[36] as well as the relatively new industry of oil extraction at Titusville, PA (fig. 11).[37] find their place also among the important resources of the country. In short, there doesn't appear to be an industrial advancement that was not depicted on the bank notes.

12

Transportation was another facet of the country's growth which found an exceptional interest with the public. A notable scene shows a vehicle similar to a Conestoga wagon passing through what appears to be a tollgate (fig. 12).[38] This scene on a note issued by the Easton and Wilkesbarre Turnpike Co. in Wilkesbarre, PA, could have taken place along one of the earliest turnpikes in the country, such as the Lancaster Pike which ran from Philadelphia to Lancaster and had tollgates every seven miles. The loading of large bales of cotton and their transportation in carts pulled by three teams of mules can be seen on bank notes issued by southern banks.[39] Their ultimate destination was the wharfs, where steamships waited in the background for the cargo brought in by carts and trains.[40]

The Black makes his appearance in these vignettes either as a cotton picker or as a driver of mule carts and coaches. The so-called Concord coach manufactured in Concord, New Hampshire seems to have been the standard means of transportation for people. One

13

vignette depicts an overland mail coach—Beachey's Line for California (fig. 13),[41] another provides a real genre scene—a friendly chat between two blacks and a white man driving a two-wheel cart.[42]

For water transportation, artists usually depicted barges as well as smaller boats and rafts. Flatboats often can be seen on large waterways. Quite interesting were the shanty boats of hunters and trappers with a hut on top for living on the water (fig. 14).[43] Hand in hand with the construction of roads came one of the most important factors in the rapid growth of the country—the development of good waterways. The first attempt to penetrate deeper into the hinterland was to connect the Hudson River with Lake Erie; conceived by Gouverneur Morris, it became a reality under the leadership of the New York Major and later Governor DeWitt Clinton (1769-1828).[44] In 1825 the Erie Canal connected Buffalo on Lake Erie with Albany on the Hudson. This success started a "canal craze or fever," which brought an undreamed expansion and prosperity to the country. The paper notes did not miss this fact. Examples include a boat drawn by horses through a canal in Washington, D.C.,[45] or in Wisconsin; [46] the James River and Kanawha Canal in

14

15

Virginia;[47] or the Dismal Swamp Canal located at the border of Virginia and North Carolina, connecting the Chesapeake Bay and Albemarle Sound.[48] Fascinating is the vignette showing the raising of a boat on a steep incline to a higher level of a canal (fig. 15).[49] Bridges varying from arched to suspension were even more often depicted on paper notes, already being shown on notes of 1816 (Bridge Co. of Augusta, Georgia). A very popular vignette used during the 1850s and 1860s is of the bridge over the Susquehanna River at Rockville, near Harrisburg, PA (fig. 16).[50]

The country seemed to have reached the peak of its mechanization through its trains, which had a slow beginning but once well

16

entrenched took over the country in a storm, helping to conquer the wide spaces of uninhabitated land and tying the Atlantic to the Pacific.

The canal era gave way to the era of trains and the paper notes reflected fully this triumph. No subject was as popular on bank notes as trains. The amazing fact is that we can follow the technical evolution of the train quite well through the vignettes, although in some cases we have to contend with the vivid imagination of the artist. After Peter Cooper proved in 1830 that his locomotive, Tom Thumb was, if not faster than the horse, at least trustworthy of negotiating treacherous curves, the future of the steam powered train was assured. Vignettes of the early 1830s show us the first trains with one or more passenger cars (fig. 17),[51] called omnibus cars, some with coal tenders,[52] others with early British engines, carrying some freight cars[53] and tenders[54] which protected the passengers from possible explosions of the boiler. Later there were trains with a John Bull locomotive, and the number of passenger and freight cars increased. The two designs from John White's book on John Bull's 150th anniversary of its first run on September 15, 1831, show the outline of the locomotive as built in 1831 by Robert Stephenson & Co., as well as its component parts, which correspond in general outlines to the drawings on our vignettes.[55] Later the outline of the steam-engine changed; in addition to a sturdier body, it had a balloon smokestack, and a cow-catcher in front.[56] Other-vignettes show us scenes in train stations;[57] the loading of mer-

17

18

chandise; people greeting the arrival of the train; and, most interesting, a freight train with many coal carts passing a coal processing factory (fig. 18),[58] symbolizing the importance trains had in the development of industry.

Ships were another principal means of transportation. Sailboats,[59] sloops, schooners, clipper ships, steamboats,[60] and Mississippi and Missouri packets and ferryboats were often depicted on paper notes. At times even the name of the more popular steamboats, such as the "Selma," could be clearly identified on the drawings.[61] The artists showed, with a tremendous pride, famous sea battles such as that of Commodore Oliver Perry's victory against the British on Lake Erie in September 1813 in an engraving by R.G. Harrison.[62] Even an ironclad cannon boat can be seen in firing position on a bank note of 1861, shortly before the famous battle between the Union's revolutionary ironclad Monitor against the ironsided Merrimack of the Confederacy. The intense water traffic had to be supplied by a booming ship construction industry, of which we find a few interesting scenes starting with notes of the late 1830s (fig. 19).[63]

19

Another important historical facet is revealed by many vignettes, i.e. the relations between two ethnical elements who were very much part of the American scene—the American Indian and the Black. Interestingly, the Indian is more often portrayed than the Black, who is usually shown as a natural aggregate of farm life (fig. 20),[64] and there appears to be no special preoccupation with the slave/owner relationship between Whites and Blacks; the latter depicted as happy and content with their way of life.[65] In this area

20

it is evident that the bank notes do not reveal any concern with the great moral and political issues of the day, slavery versus abolitionism. With the Indian the approach is quite different. The Indians seemed through their frequent portrayals and through their poses to convey a message. Their presence is acknowledged, as well as their reserve. The Indian is often a silent observer from a lonely crag of a strange civilization booming with trains, shops and beautiful buildings (fig. 21).[66] He is a hunter;[67] he enjoys his family life in the midst of natural grandeur;[68] but he does not mingle with the newcomers. Of note is that warlike poses are rarely shown.[69] Was this indeed due to the little concern shown to the Indian hostility in a period when bloody encounters raged throughout the country, or was it a rather diplomatic oversight? Do all these scenes denote the general uneasiness of the white man

21

toward the Indian? After all, most of these drawings preceded Custer's bloody end by at least 15 to 20 years. Or can it be that, within the spirit of "Manifest Destiny," the idea that the Continent was the white man's prerogative, meant that the Indian was only a part of its natural grandeur? Touching is a scene, redesigned from a less peaceful drawing, where an Indian squaw points with a conciliatory gesture toward a plow, the symbol of domesticated life (fig. 22).[70] Interesting also are some of the Indian princess's pictures,[71]

22

23

including an impressive, idealized portrait of a Madonna-like Indian huntress (fig. 23).[72]

Having examined the ethnical environment, I would like to pay some attention to the rendition of the physical environment, including a lovely view of a southern cove with beautiful palm trees and cotton plants,[73] or the rather sketchy rendition of Niagara Falls.[74] The animal world is also fairly well represented; deer, ducks, beavers, even a phoenix bird on a nest, and horses, sometimes beautiful wild horses, inspired by Le Roy's "Black and White Beauties," (fig. 24),[75] and, of course, the buffalo, the monarch of the prairies.[76] Neither do we miss man's best friend, Fido, the

24

faithful guardian of man's riches,[77] and a beautiful dog's head, copied after Edwin Landseer's painting entitled "My Dog," perhaps a Bernese Mountain Dog.[78]

Moving from the wilderness to the city, we find that bank notes often carry highly interesting urban views, some known, but many still to be identified. It is indeed fascinating to study the details of a street view in Cambridge, MA, in the 1840s,[79] or the entrance to Llowellyn Park in Orange, NJ, in 1862.[80] From among many vignettes depicting interesting buildings may be noted the very imposing view of the yet to be completed Capitol in Washington, in 1851 (fig. 25);[81] also a very interesting drawing of the old Dutch Church, built in 1815 in Albany, NY;[82] the state house in Charleston, SC,[83] and Jefferson's Monticello.[84]

25

After churches the most important buildings were banks, such as the temple-like architecture of the Girard Bank in Philadelphia,[85] or the classically inspired Bank of Louisiana in New Orleans (fig.26).[86] Boston liked to show the Bunker Hill Monument,[87] and

26

27

Baltimore depicted a slightly differently designed Battle Monument,[88] erected in 1825 in commemoration of Baltimore's defense in September 1814.

A special chapter should be devoted to the innumerable allegories, symbolizing every possible virtue and any memorable aspect of government, such as commerce or navigation. Figures such as those of Navigation[89] or Freedom and Prosperity (fig. 27)[90] are indeed very graceful and well designed. In no other group of vignettes is the influence of classical antiquity more pronounced than in the

28

29

selection of mythological and symbolical figures. The grace, attire, and coiffure of these ladies is in the finest classical tradition. They were obviously inspired or copied after classicistic paintings of good vintage as in mythological scenes depicting Neptune (fig. 28),[91] or a group of Olympians with Mercury the god of money.[92] The figure of Liberty[93] is often depicted in various attires,[94] and can be often mistaken for Columbia.[95]

Many of the support figures flanking a coat of arms refer to more up-to-date-looking people, such as workers, farmers, and women with children. Remarkable is the often encountered juxtaposition of Indians and Whites (fig. 29).[96] The importance of the Indian element in the country is acknowledged by this prestigious role assigned to them—I know of no vignettes depicting Blacks in similar poses. At the same time, through the separate grouping the artists indicated the special position assigned to the Indian in the country.

Finally, one might consider extraterrestrial figures such as an excellently executed St. George killing the dragon;[97] or Santa Claus descending from heaven to bring gifts and happiness (fig. 30).[98] I consider this unusual figure as symbolic for the entire group of vignettes, which is indeed a Santa's bag of surprises.

30

[1] Joan Dolmetsch, "Prints in Colonial America," *Prints in and of America to 1850*, Winterthur Conference Report 1970 (Charlottesville, 1970), p. 54.

[2] Sinclair Hitchings, "Graphic Arts in Colonial New England," in *Prints* (above, n. 1), p. 78.

[3] Chesterville, SC, Bank of Chester, $5, 1853.

[4] Columbia, SC, State of South Carolina, $5, 1872.

[5] Watertown, NY, The Watertown Bank & Loan Company, $10 proof, no date.

[6] Reading, PA, The Berks County Bank, $5 proof, no date.

[7] New Orleans, LA, Citizens Bank of Lousiana, $100 proof, no date.

[8] Augusta, GA, Bank of Augusta, $10, 1837.

[9] Macon, GA, Manufacturers Bank, $5, 1862.

[10] Columbia, SC, State of South Carolina, $5, 1872.

[11] Northampton, PA, Northampton Bank, 10 Taler, 1835.

[12] Savannah, GA, The Merchants & Planters Bank of the State of Georgia, $2, 1857.

[13] Smethport, PA, The McKean County Bank, $5 proof, 1858.

[14] Augusta, GA, Augusta Insurance & Banking Company, $1, 1861; see also Savannah, GA, Bank of the State of Georgia, $1, 1860.

[15] Pontiac, MI, The Bank of Pontiac, $1, 1863.

[16] De Soto, NE, The Coin Exchange Bank, $2, 1860.

[17] Towanda, PA, The Towanda Bank, $10, 1841.

[18] Savannah, GA, The Merchants & Planters Bank, State of Georgia, $2, 1859.

[19] Lexington, NC, The Bank of Lexington, $10, 1860.

[20] Helena, MT, The People's National Bank, $5 proof, no date.

[21] Jacksonville, FL, Bank of St. Johns, $5, 1859; see also, Wadesborough, NC, The Bank of Wadesborough, $10, 1859.

[22] Savannah, GA, The Timber Cutter's Bank, $1, 1858.

[23] Savannah, GA, The Bank of Commerce, $50, 1861.

[24] Dalton, GA, Planters & Mechanics Bank of Dalton, $1, 1856.

[25] Warren, PA, The North Western Bank, $5, 1861.

[26] Louisville, KY, People's Bank of Kentucky, $2, 1862.

[27] Ann Arbor, MI, The Bank of Washtenaw, $2, 1854.

[28] Newark, NJ, Newark Banking & Insurance Co., $2, 1822.

[29] Wadesborough, NC, The Bank of Wadesborough, $5, 1860.

[30] Wilmington, NC, The Bank of Cape Fear, $5, 1858.

[31] Plainfield, NJ, The Plainfield Bank, $3, 1843.

[32] Perth Amboy, NJ, Commercial Bank of New Jersey, $5, 1856.

[33] Macon, GA, Manufacturers Bank, $5, 1862.

[34] Boston, MA, The Lafayette Bank, $20, 1837.

[35] Philadelphia, PA, Manual Labor Banking House, $10, 1836.

[36] Cumberland, MD, Allegany County Bank, $5, 1862.

[37] Titusville, PA, The Petroleum Bank, $5, 1863.

[38] Wilkesbarre, PA, Easton & Wilkesbarre Turnpike Company, $1, 1816.

[39] Columbus, GA, Bank of Columbus, $1, 1856.

[40] Norfolk, VA, The Exchange Bank of Virginia, $1, 1863.

[41] Idaho City, Idaho Territory, First National Bank of Idaho, $50 proof, no date.

[42] Greensborough, GA, Bank of Greensborough, $1, 1858.

[43] Savannah, GA, Bank of Commerce, $20, 1857.

[44] Manchester, VT, Battenkill Bank, $5, 1848.

[45] Washington, DC, 12 1/2 cents, 1837.

[46] Howard, WI, The Northern Bank, $1 proof, no date.

[47] Richmond, VA, The James River & Kanawha Company, $5 proof, no date.

[48] Millington, MD, Commercial Bank, $5, 1840.

[49] Jersey City, NJ, Morris Canal & Banking Company, $10, 1838.

[50] Adrian, MI, The Adrian Insurance Company, $30, no date.

[51] Sault Ste. Marie, MI, Bank of Chippeway, $2, 1838.

[52] Ann Arbor, MI, Bank of Washtenaw, $1, 1834.

53 Augusta, GA, The Mechanics' Bank of Augusta, $1, 1854.

54 Tecumseh, MI, The Tecumseh Bank, $1 proof, no date.

55 John H. White, ***The John Bull 150 Years a Locomotive*** (Washington, DC, 1981), pp. 18 and 28.

56 Memphis, TN, The Mechanics Bank of Memphis, $1, 1854.

57 Keokuk, IA, Keokuk, Mt. Pleasant & Muscatine Rail Road, $3, 1871.

58 Elizabethport, NJ, Manufacturers Bank, $1 proof, no date.

59 Savannah, GA, Bank of Commerce, $1, 1861.

60 Brandon, MS, The Mississippi & Alabama Rail Road Company, $20, 1837.

61 Memphis, TN, The Citizens Bank of Nashville & Memphis, $1, 1856.

62 New Salem, OH, The Jefferson Bank of New Salem, $3, 1817; see also John Muscalus, ***Birch's Painting of Perry's Victory on Lake Erie Used on State Bank Notes and Scrip*** (Bridgeport, PA, 1966).

63 East Haddam, CT, The Bank of New England at Goodspeed's Landing, $5 proof, no date.

64 Macon, GA, The Manufacturers Bank, $20, 1862.

65 Montgomery, AL, Central Bank of Alabama, $50, 1859.

66 Ringgold, GA, The North Western Bank of Georgia, $10, 1861.

67 Detroit, MI, The State Bank of Michigan, $2 proof, no date.

68 Ocoee, TN, Ocoee Bank, $2, 1859.

69 Omaha City, Nebraska Territory, The City of Omaha, $1, 1857.

70 Petersburg, IN, Farmers & Drovers Bank, $10, 1858.

71 Dalton, GA, The Bank of Whitfield in Dalton, $2, 1860.

72 New Orleans, LA, Bank of Louisiana, $100, 1852.

73 Savannah, GA, Bank of Commerce, $50, 1861.

74 Battle Creek, MI, Bank of Battle Creek, $2 proof, no date.

75 Smethport, PA, McKean County Bank, $2 proof, no date.

76 Lockport, IL, State Bank of Illinois, $2.50, 1841.

77 Lowell, MA, Appleton Bank, $500 proof, no date.

[78] New Britain, CT, New Britain Bank, $1, 1863.

[79] Cambridge, MA, The Cambridge Bank, $3, 1842.

[80] Orange, NJ, Mercantile Bank, $1, 1862.

[81] Augusta, GA, Augusta Insurance & Banking Company, $100, 1860.

[82] Albany, NY, The City of Albany, 50 cents, 1862.

[83] Charleston, SC, Bank of the State of South Carolina, $2 proof, no date.

[84] Charlottesville, VA, The Monticello Bank, $20, 1860.

[85] Philadelphia, PA, Mechanics Bank, $5, 1853.

[86] New Orleans, LA, Bank of Louisiana, $20, 1862.

[87] Boston, MA, Webster Bank, $5, 18—(?).

[88] Baltimore, MD, Western Bank of Baltimore, $5, 1842.

[89] Columbus, GA, Bank of St. Mary's, $10, 1846.

[90] Fayetteville, NC, The Bank of Clarendon, $5, 1861.

[91] Millington, MD, Commercial Bank, $5, 1840.

[92] Augusta, GA, Mechanics' Bank of Augusta, $50, 1854.

[93] Savannah, GA, Bank of the State of Georgia, $5, 1855.

[94] Augusta, GA, The City Bank, $2, 1841.

[95] Hamburg, SC, Bank of Hamburg, $100, 1859.

[96] Washington, NC, Bank of Washington, $4, 1860.

[97] Augusta, GA, The City Bank, $2, 1861.

[98] New York, NY, Saint Nicholas Bank, $2, 1862.

Collecting Trends in Obsolete American Currency

Grover C. Criswell

Coinage of the Americas Conference
at The American Numismatic Society, New York

By the time I started in the paper money business some 40 years ago, it seemed that the trend already was to collect everything. It certainly is true that paper collectors collected then and continue to be interested in forming either broad or specific collections from what is available.

Already in the early 1800s, people were actually collecting colonial and continental currency that had been issued in the previous 40-50 year period. Then in the early 1820s, banks began issuing notes of their own, the designs of which were rather simple in nature but nevertheless bank notes issued by the banks themselves. The beautiful bank notes started appearing about the 1830s and increasingly by the end of the 1850s which was probably the high point of the bank note engravers' era in the United States. Some of the most beautiful bank notes, some of the most beautiful engraving work in the world, was turned out by the various bank note companies in the 1850s. Of course, these emissions opened up entirely new areas of collecting interest.

Regional Collecting

For many years in the late 1800s, people collected things just from certain areas, perhaps their own state or things they ran across locally. There was not a great amount of publicity about bank notes in those days and because they were considered of little value, the bank notes remained tucked away not to be found for another 50 years or so. It wasn't until the 1940's or actually the 1950s that one started seeing paper collected by broad areas become popular. Confederate currency is perhaps the exception since it had always been collected popularly just as colonial and continental issues had. Confederate currency was collected as early as the 1870-1880 period with the first albums on Confederate currency appearing in 1870. The popularity of Confederate currency extended to that block known as Southern States currency as well.

In the 1940s, collectors started getting interested in other areas: midwesterners became interested in midwestern notes; New Englanders in New England notes; then, rapidly, New Englanders interested in western notes and similar developments in other places as people developed interest in collecting areas.

By the 1950s the trend had begun to change again somewhat. The areas of interest began to be refined so we found people collecting notes of particular cities or towns, people collecting notes depicting railroads or other specific subjects. This expanded further into special interest areas such as educational notes; even depression scrip began to be popular in the 1950s. By the late 1950s, after numerous fine monographs by John A. Muscalus (probably the most published person on the subject of bank notes) began to circulate and be put in various numismatic libraries, more and more people became interested in the variety of collecting opportunities in bank notes. Julian Blanchard, D. O. Barrett, and Fred Markoff were three of the pioneers who collected in specialized areas such as vignettes and designs and proofs. D. O. Barrett donated his beautiful collection to Boys Town in Nebraska. In fact they built a beautiful museum there where the collection is tied in to a name that he coined—philamatic—meaning philatelic and numismatic. Julian Blanchard, after whom the principal award of the Paper Money Society is named, also exhibited extensively in areas that had not previously been popular. For instance, tieing in vignette designs with proofs and showing the entire process from the engraving of the plates, the progressive engravings and proofs—the type of thing so beautifully done today by Glenn Jackson and Walter Allen, among others, who currently display at various conventions.

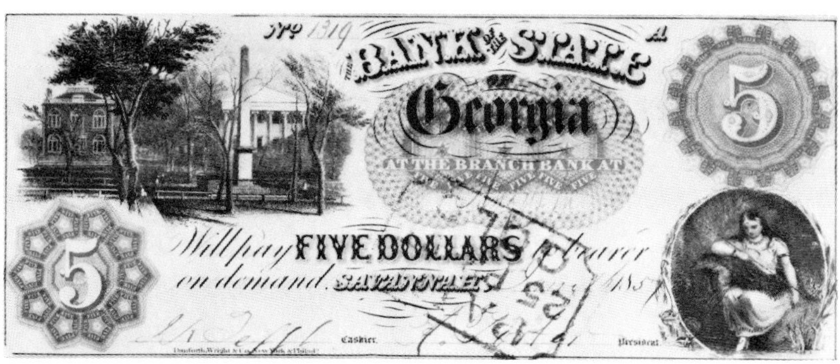

1. Savannah, GA, Bank of the State of Georgia, $5, 1857; together with proof of the left vignette.

Diversity of Collecting Opportunities

National bank notes also began enjoying increased popularity in the 1950s. National bank notes were a lot easier to find from a lot of cities and towns so people started collecting them for their local interest. I have always thought it strange that some people only collect national bank notes. To my mind, if you are interested in money issued in a city or town, you ought to be interested in the obsolete bank notes as well because they certainly preceded the national bank notes. It makes good sense from a collecting standpoint as well since someday the rarer obsoletes are going to be worth a lot more than those national bank notes which were issued in comparatively large quantities.

It wasn't unusual prior to the federal banking laws of 1863 for a variety of merchants to issue their own money: the real-life butcher, baker and candlestick maker went to the local printer and had, say, 100 pieces each of 10 cent and 25 cent notes printed. Our merchant would bring them back and hand sign, number and issue the notes, and they might be all that was issued. Naturally these are rarer than national bank notes; and some of them survived and some didn't.

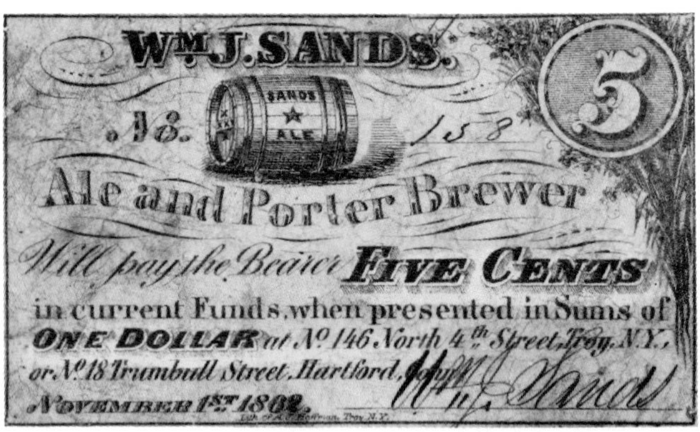

2. Troy, NY, Wm. J. Sands, 5 cents, 1862.

Finally by the late 1960s it got expensive to collect areas encompassing an entire state or the entire midwest or all of New England or other large areas. Naturally, the specialized areas then developed more rapidly. You can still put together a collection of obsolete bank notes practically any way your heart desires. You can collect railroad trains, enjoy putting together a collection for a nominal investment and have all the fun of trying to identify those trains, most of which actually can be identified. Similarly with ships and other interesting scenes, reproductions of famous paintings, famous personages, as well as coins, horses, dogs, whaling scenes, just about virtually everything. In fact, if you don't want to collect notes from a cer-

3. Jamaica, VT, The West River Bank, $3, ca. 1855 (unissued).

tain area or of certain scenes, you can collect them by colors! I know someone who collects just blue $3 bills. He's only got about 14 pieces in his collection but he's having fun—he probably has the largest collection in the world of blue $3 bills.

Another way to collect bank notes that has become pretty popular in the last few years is by denominations, often odd denominations. Some denominations are rare, such as the 11 cents or $6, 7, 8, 9, but the $11, $12, $13, $14 are even rarer. Odd denominations are often explainable. A $65 note was issued by the Brunswick and Florida Steamboat and Stage Line; $65 happened to be the total

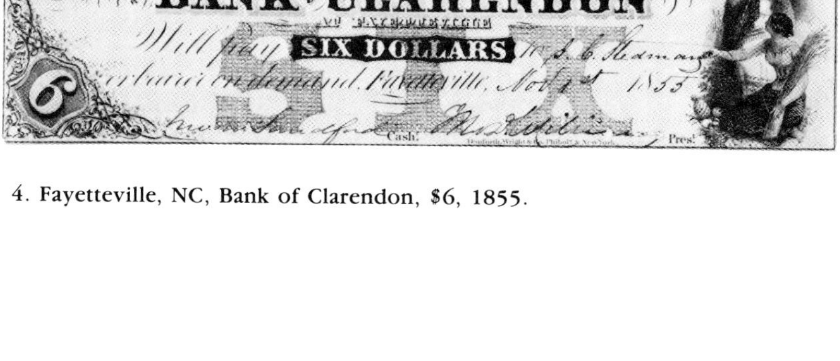

4. Fayetteville, NC, Bank of Clarendon, $6, 1855.

round trip fare. We can expect that there is somewhere a $32.50 bill which was for a half fare and there might even be a $16.25 note as well. The circulation of Spanish coins along with the U.S. in the 1840s and 1850s is the reason we find a one bit note, 12 1/2 cents, as well as the 25 cent note, and there was even a reason for the issuance of a 37 1/2 cent note—even more so, perhaps, than the issuance of a 40 cent note. An interesting facet of collecting these odd denomination notes is to seek out the reasons for their issuance.

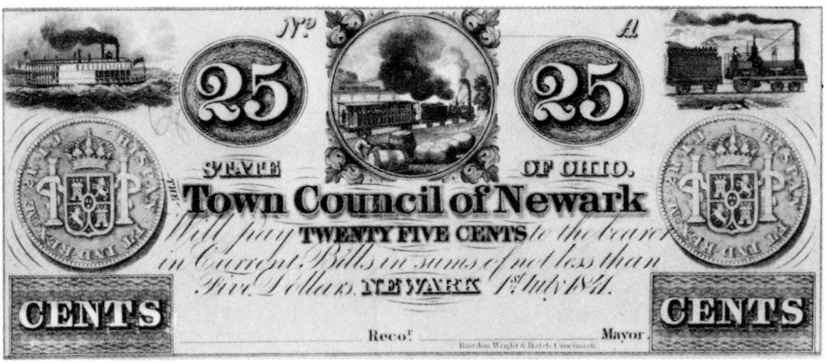

5. Newark, OH, Town Council of Newark, 25 cents (2 bits), 1841 (unissued).

Sometimes people collect notes by signature, and sometimes they collect just counterfeits of geniune notes. There are also people who are starting to collect advertising notes—ads printed on genuine bank notes, or advertisments printed in imitatiion of bank notes. These are all collectible now. It is good to keep in mind that a lot of bank notes that we consider very good, beautiful, rare and highly collectible today, probably were in somebody's junk box at some time. The collecting trend is toward more and more of everything as more and more knowledge becomes available on these items, creating the demand and also providing the impetus to turn up further material in private hands.

Last but not least, I want to say a word about condition. I would advise against the attitude in bank note collecting of only accepting bills in very fine or better condition. The note you turn down may be the only one in existence. I always advise people that if you have a hole in your collection, and you see a note that will fill it, go ahead and buy it and put it in. If you find a better one later, don't worry, you'll be able to get rid of that old duplicate, but don't set a standard for yourself that is going to preclude your picking up a great rarity. I know a lot of people that did that over the years and they sure are sorry now that they let a lot of those nice pieces go by.

An Introduction to Obsolete American Currency

Roger H. Durand

Coinage of the Americas Conference
at The American Numismatic Society, New York

The earliest bank that operated under a state charter was the Bank of North America, chartered in Pennsylvania in March 1784. Several other banks obtained state charters within the next few years, mostly in New England and New York. The first notes were crude with little or no design at all. The earliest designs were simple, such as a plain eagle, an anchor, or a simple building. As time went on, the engravers improved their trade and the vignettes became a little more complex including allegorical scenes which were frequently indefinite as to their representations. The early engravers usually did not sign their work. In some cases, engraving was just a sideline or a means to support themselves. William Hamlin, an early engraver from Providence, RI, was a man of many talents. He was an inventor and one of his trades was printing. Engraving bank note plates followed.

Within a few months of the death of George Washington, the Washington Bank of Westerly was chartered by the State of Rhode Island. It opened for business August 22, 1800. It commissioned Amos Doolittle of New Haven, CT, to engrave bank note plates with a vignette of George Washington on each denomination note. Doolittle was an excellent line engraver but his talent was sadly lacking as far as vignettes were concerned. He could not duplicate the bust of Washington repeatedly so each note on the plates renders Washington slightly differently. These were the first notes in the U.S. to use George Washington as a central vignette.

Sample submitted by the engraver Amos Doolittle for aproval by the officers of the Washington Bank of Westerly.

In the early 1800s note engraving began to improve rapidly. Early engravers such as Abner Reed and Peter Maverick quickly improved on their trade. Also, a new process for engraving bank note plates was invented by Jacob Perkins. Busts of famous Americans adorned many notes from banks all over the east coast. Full scenes were now being engraved. Allegorical figures were exact representations of who they were supposed to be, such as Neptune, Liberty, Ceres, etc. Early buildings were represented accurately such as the first State House in Newport, then the capital of Rhode Island. Peter Maverick was probably the best of the engravers of the time. Full vignettes, in some instances covering half the note, now became commonplace. William Horton did some excellent work. Engravers now signed their work. By the 1830s, the engraving was magnificent and color began to be incorporated in the design of the notes. the first color was used for a protector device such as F I V E in red over the design of the entire note. This was done to foil racketeers from raising the denomination of the note by placing higher denominations over the dies on the corners of the notes. A little later, by the 1850s and early 1860s the notes were completely colored with as many as four colors being used and were actually works of art in their own right.

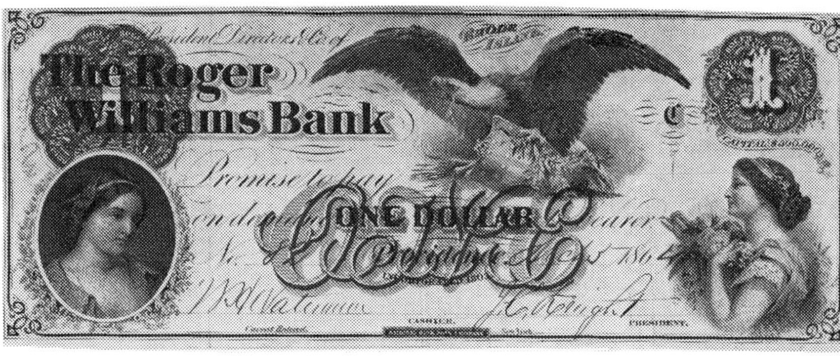

Notes were decorated with every subject imaginable. They accurately portrayed scenes of entire towns. History was recorded by these scenes. In some cases, scenes remain exactly as they were in 1850 when they were recorded on the bank notes. The Manufacturers Bank of Pawtucket, RI, pictures Samuel Slater's famous loom which he built from memory because Great Britain would allow no plans out of the country. Even Slater himself is portrayed on notes from the Slater Bank of North Providence, RI. Controversies, such as two different designed entrances to the Arcade Building in Providence, were recorded on these notes. Many famous people and some not so famous were used to embellish bank notes. The president of the American Bank of Providence, RI, Henry P. Franklin, has his portrait on all denominations of notes from his bank. His bust was identified from a family portrait; otherwise, no one would have known whose portrait was on those notes. As I have previously noted, almost any subject was put on notes of that era, even Santa Claus. He even had his own bank, the Saint Nicholas Bank of the City of New York. A vignette of Santa Claus was put on every denomination from that bank. His vignette was used on notes of several other banks as well. These notes are highly regarded and sought after by collectors.

Banks and other note issuing companies used several different denominations on their currency. Notes in the denominations of $1.25, $1.50 and $1.75 were issued from several banks. Remember,

4 $1.25 notes made change for a $5 bill, and 2 $1.50 made change for a $3 bill which was very common in this era. $2.50 notes made change for $5 or $10 bills. Even $4 bills were not uncommon. Some very unusual denominations were printed, such as $7, $14, and even a $65 bill was in use during these times. Denominations such as $1,000 were usually used for interbank transactions. Large denominations such as this were beyond the means of the average working man whose weekly salary was just a few dollars.

Since this country was inhabited by immigrants from many different countries, some of our paper money had a foreign influence incorporated on the notes. A bank from the German section of Philadelphia printed its notes in German. Spanish Pillar dollars were pictured on notes from several banks. These coins circulated along with U.S. silver dollars at the time. Great Britain also influenced some of our notes such as a note from the Washington Bank of Westerly good for 11 cents or 8 pence. This foreign flavor just adds to the pleasure of collecting obsolete bank notes.

Another interesting topic for collecting obsolete bank notes was the notes issued by territories before they became states. In some cases, the territories themselves issued notes. Companies that operated a business in the territory issued notes and in a few cases even banks operated in a territory. Banks operated under a territorial charter or in some cases, without a charter at all. The people in those outlying areas were desperate for a means to conduct commerce, especially when coinage was in short supply. Territorial Nationals are very popular with collectors while the obsolete territorials go unnoticed in most cases.

• Literally hundreds of merchants issued private scrip with no backing but their good faith. It was mostly issued in emergency situations to alleviate the need for small change. This scrip was issued in many very unusual denominations, created for specific situations. Denominations ranged from one mill to one dollar with many odd denominations in between. A note was issued for six cents and 3 mills by the Hartford and New Haven Turnpike. This note was for the passage of a one-horse sleigh. Other denominations were used for different types of traffic. A 24 cent note was issued by a New Orleans postmaster for change for an unknown type of transaction. Common denominations, such as 5, 10, and 25 cents were plentiful and in some cases, colorful works of art like the bank notes of that era. By the way, Santa Claus also appeared on a scrip note from New York. This note was worth 25 cents toward the purchase of a book about Saint Nicholas. A railroad issued notes in the odd denomination of 33 1/3 cents toward a meal on the train. I have recorded almost 100 different denominations on obsolete notes.

Our nation's early history can be traced through vignettes used to decorate the paper money of the times. Early historical events from the landing of Columbus up to and including scenes of the Civil War were used on obsolete bank notes. The most popular historical event was the signing of the Declaration of Independence. Several banks used this vignette on their notes. Other historical events, such as the Battle of Bunker Hill are rarely depicted and are only to be found on one bank note or perhaps on notes from just one or two banks. Different engraving companies portrayed the same historical event differently. Each artist had his own interpretation of how the event took place. Several versions of the battle of New Orleans appear on notes from banks in several states. The version by the American Bank Note Company is a superb example of the battle scene.

The formation of states throughout the country caused many problems.One problem that affected banking and our early paper money was boundary changes. A good example of the problems this caused is found on a note from the Pawtucket Bank of Pawtucket, MA. In 1860 the northern portion of Pawtucket became part of Rhode Island. At the same time, Fall River, RI became part of Massachusetts. Bank notes exist from the Pocasset Bank dated in Rhode Island and then, later on, dated in Massachusetts. Boundary changes in several other states make the collecting of these notes interesting.

The predominant problem that occurred during the state bank era was counterfeiting. Banks as well as their clientele were constantly harassed by fraudulent notes. There were several types of deceptive bank notes. Counterfeits which were supposed to be a duplicate of a genuine bank note were abundant. Several banks went into receivership due to poor management and in some cases, outright fraud. Their notes became worthless. They were acquired by counterfeiters who obliterated the city or both the city and state and changed the location to an existing bank which was still in operation. Many were so skillfully done that they fooled even the most cautious person. Another type of counterfeiting problem was the raising of the denomination of the bank note. A genuine $1 bill would have the counters either obliterated or a piece from another higher denomination bill glued over the original counter. Therefore, a $1 could have been passed as a $10 or $20 bill. Still another form of a counterfeit note was a spurious note made from a plate that was never used by the bank. The same plate would be used to print notes of several banks by just changing the bank title, location or some other aspect of the note. As a means to give a form of credibility, the signatures were supposed to represent the actual officers of the bank. A good example of this type of fraud is the $5 bill from the Manufacturers Bank of Providence, RI signed and dated May 1, 1842 supposedly by Samuel Slater as President. Samuel Slater died in 1835.

The first bank to fail was the Farmers Exchange Bank of Glocester, RI. It was incorporated in February, 1804 and closed on March 24, 1809. This failure caused a chain reaction of other bank failures including the Coos Bank in New Hampshire. These and a few other banks were wholly owned and controlled by Andrew Dexter, Jr. who in a short time put into circulation over $650,000 of currency which was a total loss to bill holders. When the bank failed, its tangible assets were $86.46 while it had about $580,000 in bills outstanding. A legislative committee of Rhode Island in 1830 destroyed, by authority, $81,500 in bills of his bank. The common term by which these notes from the states bank era are known is broken bank note although several hundred banks did not go broke as the term implies. The last bank to surrender its state charter, at least in Rhode

Island, was the High Street Bank. It continued to operate under a state charter during the entire National Bank period and redeemed its state bank notes right up to end of its state bank era. It surrendered its state charter in 1930 and is today known as the Citizens Bank. We began this discussion with the Washington Bank of Westerly, RI, so it only seems fitting to end by noting that to this very day, this bank will still redeem its notes at par after almost 200 years of continuous operation.

The Financial Concerns of a Government Employee in the 1840s

Cory Gillilland

Coinage of the Americas Conference
at The American Numismatic Society, New York

An account book is like a financial diary; and like other diaries, some items probably are forgotten or simply omitted. Yet, there is retained a flavor of the economic conditions experienced by the keeper of the account.

Lewis H. Machen, Clerk in the United States Senate for almost half of the nineteenth century, kept such financial diaries. His meticulous accounts of his own expenses and those of his family, together with voluminous quantities of correspondence retained over the years, provide valuable information about his financial concerns and the time in which he lived.

These accounts are particularly interesting to those studying the United States economy before 1863, as Lewis Machen's life spanned the period between the Revolutionary and the Civil Wars. He was born in 1790, several years before the appearance of a United States Mint and United States coinage. He died in 1863 during the height of the Civil War and only months after the passage of the National Currency Act. In short, his life encompasses the age of experimental banking in this country.

Machen's chief claim to fame during his lifetime came about because of his being in the right place at the right time. Due to a change in residence in 1814 brought about as a result of his constant aim to supplement his income, Machen was not with the militia on the Monday preceding the British attack on Washington. He, therefore, reported to work on Capitol Hill where it was left to him to remove the important documents from the Capitol. With great difficulty, he transported the confidential and executive proceedings of the Senate to safety. He later wrote, "these constituted, at that time, the only evidence in existence of the executive doings and votes of the Senate for a period of twenty-five years."[1]

Machen saved many scraps of paper relating to his own expenditures. Personal accounts of the variety usually discarded by most people throughout history now exist as documents which provide a general feeling for the expenses incurred by a family living in the nineteenth century. These papers may be particularly noteworthy for those studying agriculture and farm labor as the Machen family kept weekly records of farm activities and expenses. There are two separate one-year periods which are of particular interest because they provide an account of prices during the time and of the difficulties imposed by the banking situation. From August 1842 to August 1843, while the family was living in Washington, D. C. on

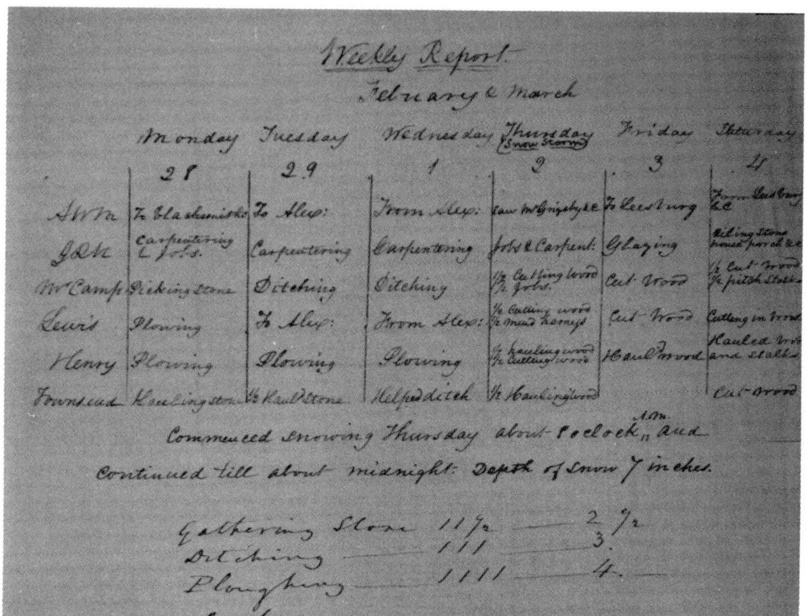
Weekly Report
February & March
Monday 28 | Tuesday 29 | Wednesday 1 | Thursday 2 (Snow Storm) | Friday 3 | Saturday 4
Commenced snowing Thursday about 8 o'clock A.M. and continued till about midnight: Depth of snow 7 inches.
Gathering Stone 11½ — 2½
Ditching 111 — 3.
Ploughing 1111 — 4.

a government employee's salary, Lewis Machen kept fairly complete records of his expenses and those of his wife and three children. During a second one-year period, August 1845 to August 1846, when Lewis Machen was working in the city and his family was living at Walney Farm in Fairfax County, Virginia, he again kept accounts of both his expenses and of those living on the farm. The records of the other years are not as all inclusive as these two mentioned.

Before discussing the family expenses, one should first have a clearer image of Lewis Machen, of who he was, and what he did for a living. Shortly after the death of his parents in 1810, Lewis Machen, then twenty years old, secured a position as Engrossing Clerk in the Office of the Secretary of the United States Senate at a yearly salary of $1,000.[2] Working under the Principal Clerk, Machen and another junior clerk acted as the administrative managers of the Senate floor and as the facilitators of legislation. Today these functions within the Office of the Secretary are handled by the offices of the Assistant Secretary, the Bill Clerk, the Enrolling Clerk, the Executive Clerk, the Journal Clerk, and the Legislative Clerk, all of whom earn yearly incomes in the vicinity of $68,000.

When Machen began, the Senators themselves were paid $6 a day when present. From 1815 through 1817 they were paid $1,500 annually.[3] By comparison, those who put the Senators' words into print, the compositors and the pressmen, earned each year a little over one half that paid to Machen. During a recess of Congress they received not less than $9 per week and during the session not less than $10 per week, with an additional $2 for each and every Sunday. This was the occupational scale in Washington from 1815 to about 1835.[4] In other words, Lewis Machen as a young man earned a salary almost double that of a skilled craftsman in the employment of the U. S. Senate. By comparison with other parts of the country, Machen himself discovered that he made $250 more than a judge in Kentucky.[5]

It is through Machen's correspondence that one gains an impression of this man who daily was in contact with those whose persuasions shaped our nation. Throughout his nearly fifty-year career in the Senate he came into contact with statesmen of the Revolutionary period, the antebellum age, and with those of the Civil War era. His letters speak of the eloquent debates of John Randolph and Charles Pinckney, of the establishment of a National Bank, of Henry Clay's speaking abilities, of the views of Chief Justice Marshall, Daniel Webster, John C. Calhoun and others.

After the early death of his first wife and his second marriage to Caroline Webster, Lewis Machen moved to a rented house in

Washington City. To the extent that he was financially able, he dealt in real estate to supplement his income. In about 1820 he purchased half of a "square" bounded by Maryland Avenue, 10th, 11th and C streets, Southwest, for $2,775. A year later he built a house on this half acre lot at a cost of $4,585.89. This location is now the site of the multi-million dollar L'Enfant Plaza" Typical of Machen, he retained all bills for later improvements on his house so that at the end of his family's twenty-year stay, the records show the brick home itself had cost $5,775.13.[6]

During the time that Machen was building his home, there is indication that he had income other than his salary. For example, during the months of April and June 1823, he deposited $1,420.55 in notes for collection in the Bank of Washington. This no doubt came from real estate activities. The deposits made in cash during the same period amounted to only $161. The total deposits were $1,581.55. The memorandum of deposit states the name of the drawer of each note and the endorser. One must remember that this was twenty years before the first clearing house was established in this country. The amount of cash in this one small example is only 10.1 percent of the two months' deposit.

Although occupied with his job and his outside financial tasks during his life in Washington, Machen did find time for politics and writing. In 1828 he was reprimanded by the Secretary of the Senate, Walter Lowrie, for publishing articles in the press under an assumed name in support of John Quincy Adams, a Whig and an anti-Jackson candidate. Machen replied that his long service had been exemplary and that his right as a private citizen allowed an expression of his sentiments on the public topics of the day. the deomocrats, however, were elected and when he aspired to the post of Secretary of the Senate, Machen found few Senators in support. Somehow he retained his clerkship and in 1836 was even promoted to Principal Clerk at a yearly salary of $1,800.[7]

During this difficult period for Machen, he had the added expense of having his oldest child, Emmeline, in boarding school at the Greenfield High School for Young Ladies in Massachusetts. A bill dated February 13, 1835, records that the board and instruction for one quarter, including stationery, was $37.50. Extra board of one and one half weeks cost $3.75. To this amount was added $2 for music practice without lessons, $4 for Latin instruction, $6 for drawing and painting instruction, and $1 for the entrance fee in music. The bill for the term came to $54.25. During her absence from home, "Emme" wrote regularly to the family and often included discussions of her finances. She wrote in a letter dated December 8, 1839, that her bonnet cost $8.50. A band box was $3, and she paid $1 to a seamstress or mantilla maker, who at the time was buying two papers of needles for 25 cents. In spite of such expenses, Lewis Machen continued to enter into outside financial obligations. In 1839 he purchased three shares of Chesapeake and Ohio Canal Company Stock. That same year the State of Maryland paid $1,000 per share for stock in this company.[8]

In the early 1840s, Machen's son Arthur also was in boarding school. Enrolled in Columbian College, now George Washington University, Arthur's summer term payment was $18.25. This included room, furniture, library, and a servant! The winter term bill was $44.90.

An account of a New York City trip for the whole family in the summer of 1840, the year the Independent Treasury Act became law, is particularly illuminating. Boarding for the Machen family in the Mansion House at 39 Broadway was a dollar a day for 23 days. Arthur's diary described the location as "a fine hotel on Broadway and but a short distance from the steamboat landing."[9] The least amount included in the accounting was 25 cents paid to the baggage porter to bring the luggage from the harbor. The complete excursion cost Machen $168.66. This included the $38 fare from Washington to New York for the family, and $10 for a side trip to New Hampshire, his wife's home.

In 1841 Lewis Machen began to comtemplate the purchase of a farm in Virginia. He was offered a 330 acre farm for "$10,000 with a 10 percent discount allowed if paid in cash or for such portion as would be appropriated to the payment of certain back debts...."[10]

Machen delayed making this decision. One account of that time states that the interest rate on a $50 loan which he repaid was 6 percent.[11] He no doubt was concerned about the fiscal and banking situation in the country. After the August 1841 rejection of the Fiscal Bank bill to establish the Fiscal Bank of the U. S. in Washington, DC, he wrote to his son:

> The last week has been of great interest in our city. A week elapsed last Saturday since the Bank Bill was forwarded to the President for approval. It was considered today. The Bill and its provisions were defended by Mr. Clay. The President's course was supported by Mr. Rives and few occasions within my recollection have been more exciting or have called forth more debating talent...The rejection will probably lead to the introduction of another Bank Bill, more in conformity to the

> views of the President and I am apprehensive we cannot adjourn in less than 18 days.[12]

That same month a uniform bankruptcy law went into effect whereby a person could voluntarily declare bankruptcy. During the three-year tenure of this law, 33,737 people took advantage of it. Mr. Beverly C. Sanders, a wholesale grocer in Baltimore, wrote to Machen a year after the passage of the bill, "the Bankrupt law has done its worst, and all the benefits which were to flow from it to creditors is just commencing."[13]

Lewis Machen's apprehension of the country's fiscal condition, however, did not prevent him from purchasing what would seem a luxury. In November of 1841 he itemized the five installments totaling $600 paid for the family house slave, Lucy.[14]

Fiscal debates continued both in the United States Congress and in private. At the beginning of the next year, 1842, Machen's friend Sanders wrote again from Baltimore:

> In consequence of the damaged condition of the currency, the increasing evils of selected circulation and the partial action of the Legislature, it will not be possible for me to leave home until some definite action is had on these matters. The Chesapeake Bank paper is refused by other banks. Clark, the broker, and banker has absconded since 12 o'clock today, and there is considerable excitement in the city.
>
> This is truly a time of great trial and difficulty within the community. Where and when it will end tis impossible even to conjecture. Certainly not while Congress continues to enact the disgraceful scenes which are daily witnessed within its halls instead of mastering the measures of relief which are so loudly called for by a suffering people.[15]

A month later, the same friend again wrote, this time interjecting his idea for a solution:

> You say truly, the situation of business men, dependent so greatly on a currency of some known and fixed value, is indeed most lamentable. I feel it every day most sensibly, and am looking forward to disasters which from present appearances seem inevitable, and which must sweep over the land like a destructive tornado leaving only the wreck of what this fair land once was. I hope the gloomy forbodings will not be realized, but I am not hopeful to expect better. Until our foreign policy undergoes complete and thorough revision, and we get

> out of debt. The latter consumation depends upon the proper adjustment of the tariff laws...We find the New York market inundated with foreign goods imported by foreigners. These goods must be paid in gold and silver, and at a time, too, when we cannot pay even the interests on what we owe the foreigner. Mark the effect. In the first place whatever may be the result on the real owner of the goods to sacrifice them here at reduced rates, it is calculated to give the finished stroke to our now almost expiring manufacturings and the second place, make a still greater draw on our stock of precious metals and if the system is not checked, who will soon know what a dollar or half eagle is, only from memory. It is not pleasant. Depend upon it, this is the evil and here the work must begin. As to Bankers, Exchequer projects, sub-treasuries, treasury note bills, and all that stuff, about which the wisdom of the nation is wrangling so much. They are all collated to the main question, which must be first settled, but which will not, in my opinion, be adjusted for some time to come yet.[16]

Such was the feeling of those close to Lewis Machen. It is during this same year, 1842, that Machen kept what seems to be a fairly complete account of his family expenses in Washington, DC. From September 1, 1842, to August 12, 1843, Machen recorded a total of 1,396.11 in family expenses. This when averaged over the eleven and one half months period amounts to a monthy expenditure of $121.40. Lewis Machen's salary at his time was $150 a month.

During the first month, September 1842, the Machen family spent a total of $167.92. In order to transmit a flavor of the type of expenses encountered by the family, the following were selected from the September accounting. Machen listed "marketing" eight times during the month. The highest of these marketing costs was $1.74; the lowest was $1.05. The total monthly costs listed as "marketing" are $13.37. Throughout the year he often broke the "marketing" cost into individual expenditures. For example, he listed two pounds of butter for 63 cents, sweet potatoes for 10 cents, bread at 5 cents and 10 cents, and at another time 15 cents. He listed eight pounds of beef for 62 cents, a peck of onions at 12 cents, four eggs for 6 cents, tomatoes for 6 cents, oysters for 25 cents, twenty bushels of potatoes including hauling for $5.56, six large crooked-neck squash for 75 cents, 750 pounds of pork for $36.56, turkey for 81 cents, oranges and lemons for three days at 50 cents, molasses at 12 1/2 cents, cheese for 32 cents, two quarts of peaches for 25 cents, cream of tartar at 6 cents, a twenty-pound keg of crackers for $1, sixteen pounds of sugar for $1, tea at 25 cents, five pounds of rice for 25 cents, one red pepper for 25 cents, and twelve beef tongues for $3. A barrel of flour cost $5 and the winter's supply of butter was $23.40.

Other family items included books for the children, one on rhetoric for 87 cents, one on alegbra for $1 and a grammar book for $1. Almost the next day Machen recorded $2.75 for more books. That year a half gallon of brandy cost $1.25 and a bottle of port wine with a bottle of brown stout was obtained for $1.38. String for his son's kite was 37 1/2 cents and at one point he paid $2 for candy for his daughter. Fifty cents was given to one of the children for losing a tooth.

For himself and his two sons, the expenses mentioned included a man's frock coat at a cost of $18. A silk shirt was $2.50, men's shoes cost $2.75 while boots were $2.50. Boy's shoes were $2; a boy's summer cap was 75 cents, a winter cap cost $1.37 1/2 cents. The labor for a boy's handmade jacket amounted to 81 cents. A hair-cut cost 25 cents. Machen paid 25 cents for repairing his umbrella while at another time two new umbrellas cost $1.50. Spectacles were purchased for $1.50, shaving soap for 50 cents and a shaving brush for 37 1/2 cents. A day's cab fare cost $1 while the omnibus from Georgetown was 12 cents.

In the feminine line, a lady's shawl cost $2.50, shoes were $1.25 and gloves went for 37 cents. A woman's dress, that is, one for the domestic slave, cost $1 and her kerchief was 18 3/4 cents. Trimmings for pantaloons were secured for 75 cents.

Charity included $2 each to two different local churches. In addition, $2 was sent to a female orphanage.

Machen's taxes for 1842 were $38.55, and for his son's doctor bill he recorded $18. The dog's license cost $2, a sum remarkably comtemporary.

House expenses included an annual whitewashing at $2.50; they purchased four vegetable dishes at $1.87, two pairs of sheets for $2.20 and four loads of gravel cost $1. For topping the chimneys of the house, the laborer was paid $20.

One is given the impression from Machen's accounts that, whenever possible, the family purchased on credit and often paid with bank drafts. For example, on the first days of the month Machen often paid establishments which must have been merchants. Between September 1 and 3, 1842, he paid $19.69 to Jackson and Brothers for groceries and $6.93 to Bradley and Estep for dry goods. On the first of October he paid $38.27 to "Stillinus for clothing" for the boys. A November 1 entry lists $11 to "Hall and Brothers for James and Arthur," his sons. On December 31 he again paid Jackson and Brothers, the grocers, a sum of $39.58. On December 20 he paid $40.30 to M. Caldwell for the "bill of groceries." On May 1 Bradley Estep was again paid, this time $11.11 "for clothing for Arthur and James." The winter's supply of butter mentioned above was actually paid for in May.

For the next two years, September 1843 to September 1845, the list of family expenditures seems incomplete. The Machens were in the throes of moving their household. In May of 1843 Machen purchased 725 acres of Virginia farm land including two houses and farm buildings for $10,878.94. He paid $2,300 down, $2,000 of which was borrowed, and carried the remainder as debt for a number of years.

In June of that year, 1843, Machen sold stock for $2,650. His agent happily reported that he "got 96 percent for the stock and saved the interest due on July 1." After the expenses of transfer, Machen received $2,579.60 which he must have used toward the purchase of the farm. That same month he procured a plow from J.S. Eastman in Baltimore for $12 and began the business of running a farm in absentia.

The Machen family moved to Walney Farm and Lewis continued to work for the U.S. Senate commuting to the farm when possible. He secured the services of Hiram Deyo as overseer for $250 a year. The payments made by Machen to this man were sporatic. In November of 1843, Deyo was given $25 in three separate payments. In December there was one cash payment of $5, he received the same in March, two such payments in May, and one in August. the amount of $1.25 was subtracted at the end of the year for training and absence. In August of 1844 after working for a year, the overseer received a check on the Bank of Washington for the balance, $173.75.

Another farm laborer was contracted to work for a year at $132. He was paid small amounts at irregular intervals throughout the term. The remainder was settled by a note on demand but only after deducting the interest of 4 percent on money which he had borrowed from Machen. Other employees were obtained by hiring the services of slaves from neighboring owners. The owner of one such employee received $3 a month which Machen paid regularly in cash.

The year 1844 was one of difficulty and anxiety for the Machens. Lewis was living in a room in Washington and could go to Walney only when Congress was not in session. The family found the adjustment difficult and the financial concerns tremendous. Constant expenditures were necessary to begin the farming venture. The family letters are filled with accounts of how the $5 or the $20 Lewis sent were expended and how the family needed more to meet their bills. Again and again Machen was asked to send money for salaries. The farm loan was constantly a topic of concern. In February Mrs. Machen wrote, "The winter is slipping away rapidly, and I tremble to think how much money will be required to carry out our plans here, and meet the two next payments. I hope you get your house rent in time to meet your interest to Mr. Hill."[17]

It appears that Machen was being pressured in early 1845 to buy bonds held by Powell on Machen's farm debt. A January 10 letter from Arthur states that the court had ordered Powell to sell the bonds at par and that his family preferred that Machen rather than someone else take them. Arthur stated that if his father bought the bonds at par he would not gain much for after the next payment there would remain $4,350. However, if Powell's family would throw off $600 or even $300 something would be gained.[18] Caroline Machen urged her husband to see if such arrangements could be made. In a note written on February 8, she said, "It would be a happy thing if you could obtain the money...it would be saving something and putting the property in your hands."[19]

On August 1 of 1845, Lewis Machen's accounting of both farm and family expenses began. During the first two months the receipts totaled $404.35. This included $300 of Machen's salary for two months, $68.75 from one month's rent on their Washington house, and $35.60 received from 38 42/60 (bushels) of wheat which had been sold. Their $541.19 expenditures exceeded the two months' receipts by $136.84. These expenditures included payments on loans, as well as purchases of seed and cattle for the farm.

On October 30 Machen paid the 1845 taxes of $17.68 on his Virginia property. The 1844 taxes of $40.26 for his city property were not paid until August 25 of 1846.

Machen was carrying at least two loans at this time. To Silas Hill, the Washington financier from whom he had borrowed money to buy the farm, he was paying $60 including interest, though payments were made only in October and May. On August 1 and on September 1 he paid $103.45 to a Mr. Parker. These payments went up $1 in October and November and continued to climb $1 each payment until January of 1846.

During the next year, 1846, Machen was carrying at least five loans and was able to pay only a little at a time. He not only owed Parker and Hill but was sending $50 amounts to "curtail" the Bank of Washington and the Bank of the Metropolis. At the same time he

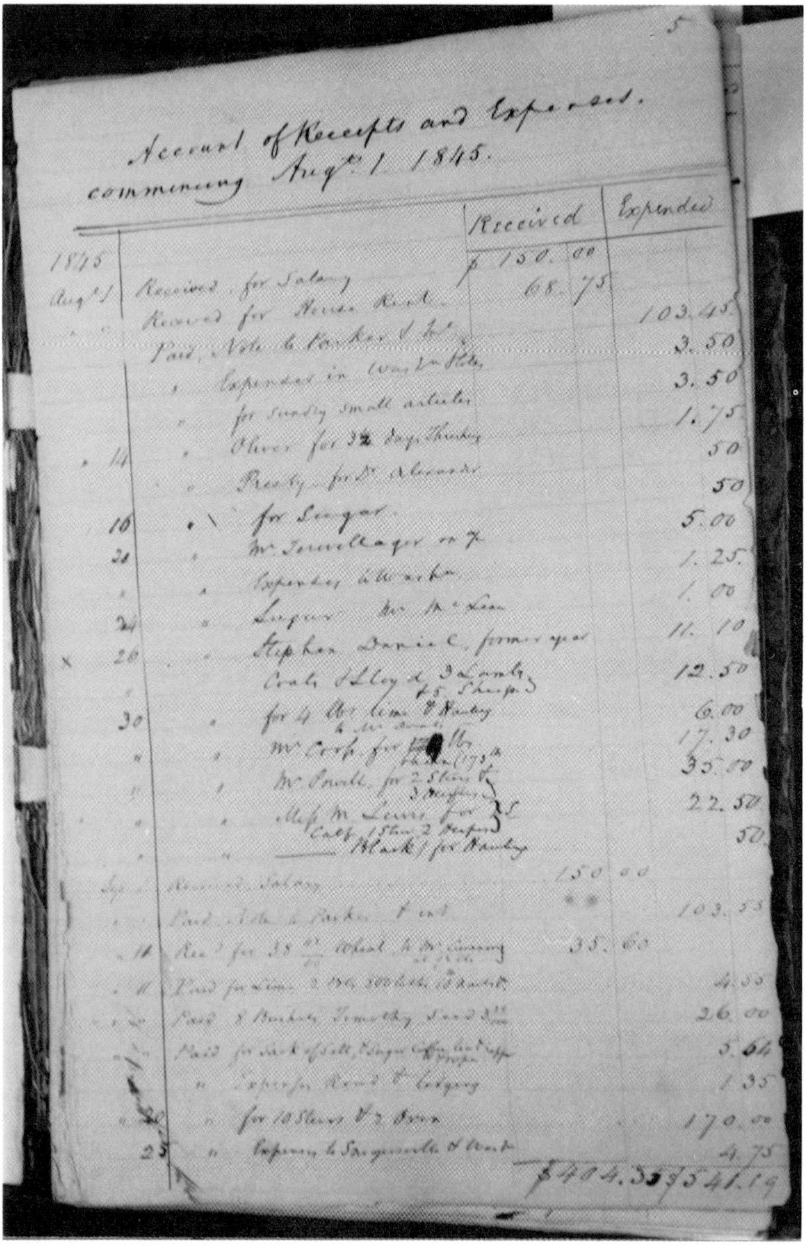

Account of Receipts and Expenses.
commencing Augt. 1 1845.

		Received	Expended
1845 Augt. 1	Received for Salary	$ 150.00	
	Received for House Rent	68.75	
	Paid, Note to Parker & Int.		103.45
	" Expenses in Washn. City		3.50
	" for Sundry small articles		3.50
	" Oliver for 3½ days Thrashing		1.75
14	" Presly for Dr. Alexander		50
	" for Sugar		50
16	" Mr. [illegible]		5.00
21	" Expenses to Washn.		1.25
	" Sugar Mr. McLean		1.00
24	" Stephen Daniel, former year		11.10
26	" Coats & Lloyd 3 Lambs & 5 Sheep		12.50
30	" for 4 Bu. Lime & Hauling		6.00
	" Mr. Cross, for [illegible]		17.30
	" Mr. Powell, for 2 Steers & 3 Heifers		35.00
	" Miss M. Lewis for Calf		22.50
	" Black for Hauling		50
Sept.	Received Salary	150.00	
	Paid Note to Parker & Int.		103.55
11	Recd. for 38 bu. Wheat to Mr. [illegible]	35.60	
11	Paid for Lime [illegible]		4.55
[illegible]	Paid 8 Bushels Timothy Seed [illegible]		26.00
	Paid for Sack of Salt, Sugar, Coffee [illegible]		5.64
	" Expenses Road & Lodging		1.35
20	" for 10 Steers & 2 Oxen		170.00
25	" Expenses to [illegible] & Wash.		4.75
		$484.35	$541.19

was making interest payments to Corcoran and Riggs.

In December of 1845 Lewis found it was impossible to be at Walney with the family. The holidays were not pleasant ones that year. Two days before Christmas Lewis Machen wrote to his wife:

> Such has been the extraordinary pressure upon the money market here produced by withdrawal from the Banks of nearly all the money on deposit in them—causing the Banks in their turn to call in all their notes as they become due and withhold further discounts even on strictly commercial sixty day paper, that Mr. Parker here informs me it is impossible for him to advance me on even a part of the sum I require. What is due from me to the Bank of Washington is required to be paid. An application to Corcoran and Riggs who alone have Deposit from the Government, and to the Bank of Metropolis, has failed—and my only dependence that on Mr. H. will I fear be attended with as little success. I shall immediately, therefore, take steps to sell my plate—retaining only what you will inform me you wish to keep—and endeavor all I can to expediate the fattening of the steers. My Bond must be over until the pressure is diminished and things resume their ordinary state.
>
> Perhaps if Arthur were to call on Cousin Lewis, she would favor him so far as to accompany him to Mr. George Carter, possibly he could lend me $1700 for a single year. I can give him personal security—an assignment of my salary with the insurance I have obtained, or a lien on my stock and library—which would sell for double the amount.
>
> At all events I wish Arthur to ride to Mr. Powell, and inform him of my disappointment, and of my determination to leave nothing undone to obtain the amount at the earliest practicable moment."[20]

In less than two weeks, on January 2, Machen paid $100 on his life insurance. Four days later he had better news and wrote to Arthur, "Tell your Ma I had yesterday to meet Mr. Powell and had the pleasure to pay him $1000, obtained from our friends—and have the assurance when the Banks do anything that I may obtain an amount sufficient to discharge my obligation."[21]

Yet on January 24, he entered into his account that he had sold the silver plate and had received $351.30 for 234 ounces of silver sold at $1.50 per ounce.

Machen somehow met his debts and held onto the farm. Arthur

wrote on June 26 that the deed of release had been delivered and that the fees for the enrollment of the property would amount to $1.50 or $2.[22]

In the middle of that busy summer, 1846, Machen, tired and not in the best of health after the long Congressional session, considered what he and the family had been through with their financial obligations to date. He wrote Arthur:

> At present the total value of all that is made with my salary in addition has done little more than pay our way. In 3 years I may have appropriated $1000 from my salary and house rent—the proof of this is that I have borrowed $7000, that I owe at least several hundred; and that I have paid for the ground $8,300. The money I had, when I began; with my *plate* and furniture sold, would have amounted to $3,600, at least; and my improvements, stock and implements would not have cost more. Can we expect to do better for the future? If not, how are the two next installments to be paid? Our wages amount to $700, family expenses for 10, not less than $750- total $1,450. Will the value we raise in this year, estimated at the farm, amount to 1,500? Here there are clothing, contingencies, Smith, taxes, with nothing to meet them.
>
> What can be done. Can we hire at less wages? Can we change our system? and make more from the land in grazing, in dairy, and in scrubs, and plough less land, and thus employ less labor?
>
> Can fewer persons be employed? and can wages be rendered less expensive?
>
> I wish you and Ma to give me *immediately*, what you think....[23]

By the end of August the Machen family had expenses for a year amounting to $3,852.22. They had received only $3,370.15. By the end of that year, Arthur was once again writing his father concerning loans. Mrs. Carter was unable to lend money to Machen "though there was no one to whom she would sooner grant the loans. However, all money coming into her hands for the next twelve months was already disposed of."[24] The year had begun with the selling of the family silver and ended with little hope for better. The bulk of their expenses for the year had been for stock and seed, for payments on loans, and for labor. Machen had made that year $1,800 in salary, $300 additional for the long Senate session, and $825 in rent from his city property—a total of $2,925. His total payments on loans and as curtailments to banks amounted to $1,583.37, or more than half of his income away from the farm. That year the farm produced $445.15.

Debts and loans, bank closings and late payments seem to have been a way of life for the family at that time. And all of this Machen was recording in the midst of constant discussions in his letters concerning the split between the states and his anxiety about the precarious state of the Union.

Later the farm seems to have prospered. In 1849 Machen was able to send his son Arthur to the Harvard Law school. In 1859, angered by the appointment in the Senate of a younger man to a higher paying position, Machen retired to Walney. His forebodings about the Union were soon realized and at the time of the first battle of Bull Run, Walney was occupied by soldiers. Lewis Machen, a Union man, moved to Baltimore to live with his son, Arthur. His younger son, James, served with Confederate troops. Only months after the passage of the National Currency Act, Lewis Machen died, leaving us with a fascinating financial record from the period of experimental banking in the United States.

[1] Lewis Machen to William C. Rives, September 12, 1836. Machen Papers, Library of Congress Manuscript Division (LCMs Div).

[2] Elizabeth Pryor, *Walney, Two Centuries of a Northern Virginia Plantation* (Fairfax County, VA, 1984), p. 34.

[3] Per interview with Richard Baker, U.S. Senate Historian, October 17, 1985.

[4] U.S. Department of Labor. *History of Wages in the United States from Colonial Times to 1928* (Washington, 1934), pp. 121-22.

[5] Arthur W. Machen, Jr., *Letters of Arthur W. Machen with Biographical Sketch* (Baltimore, 1917), p. 18.

[6] *Letters* (above, n. 5), p. 12.

[7] *Letters* (above, n. 5), p. 27.

[8] Per interview with Douglas McElrath, Maryland Hall of Records, Annapolis, October 16, 1985.

[9] Arthur Machen Journal, beginning August 1840. Machen Papers, LCMsDiv.

[10] E. Rogers to Lewis Machen, October 12, 1841. Machen Papers, LCMsDiv.

[11] Lewis Machen to Arthur. Memorandum of Payment, September 1, 1842. Machen Papers, LCMsDiv.

[12] Lewis Machen to Arthur, August 18, 1841. Machen Papers, LCMsDiv.

[13] Beverly C. Sanders to Lewis Machen, December 17, 1842. Machen Papers, LCMsDiv.

[14] Thomas Blagden to Machen. Memorandum of payment for Lucy, 1841. Machen Papers, LCMsDiv.

[15] Sanders to Machen, January 27, 1842. Machen Papers, LCMsDiv.

[16] Sanders to Machen, February 16, 1842. Machen Papers, LCMsDiv.

[17] Caroline Machen to Lewis. Postscript on letter from Arthur Machen to Lewis. Machen Papers, LCMsDiv.

[18] Arthur Machen to Lewis, January 10, 1845. Machen Papers, LCMsDiv.

[19] Caroline Machen to Lewis. Postscript on letter from James Machen to Lewis, February 8, 1845. Machen Papers, LCMsDiv.

[20] Lewis Machen to Caroline, December 23, 1845. Machen Papers, LCMsDiv.

[21] Lewis Machen to Arthur, January 5, 1846. Machen Papers, LCMsDiv.

[22] Arthur Machen to Lewis, June 26, 1846. Machen Papers, LCMsDiv.

[23] Lewis Machen to Arthur, July 8, 1846. Machen Papers, LCMsDiv.

[24] Arthur Machen to Lewis, December 4, 1846. Machen Papers, LCMsDiv.

The History and Development of 'America' as Symbolized by an American Indian Female

Gene Hessler

Coinage of the Americas Conference at The American Numismatic Society, New York

With the adoption of the Great Seal of the United States in 1782, designed by Charles Thompson, the American bald eagle became the symbol of American liberty. Official or not, the bird, which Franklin referred to as ignoble and a scavanger, was no match for the Indian maiden who for over two centuries had symbolized the new world, the Americas, to Europeans.

Most mortals need symbols to help them grasp the concept of an idea, person or place, that will probably remain only in their mind's eye. Europeans needed a symbol for America, and the "Indian Princess," occasionally called the "Indian Queen," filled that need. Although America was primarily an extension of the European mind, native Americans were viewed in duality; they were considered savages, offsprings of the devil, and conversely as Apollos or Venuses.

Following publication of Martin Waldseemüller's *Cosmographiae Introductio* in 1507, the "New World" was generally known as America. "In 1515 Albrecht Dürer drew in the margin of the Book of Hours he decorated for the Emperor Maximillian I an American Indian...."[1] About 1575 Johannes Stradanus (Jan van der Straet), drew *The Discovery of America*. Here, Amerigo Vespucci is seen arousing *America* from her *hamaca* (fig. 1). This drawing accompanied Corbeiller's comments on the much disputed discovery of America in 1497 by Vespucci.

1

Explorers who followed Columbus and Vespucci to the Western Hemisphere, all of which was referred to as America between 1575 and 1765, returned with plants, animals and natives, heretofore unknown to Europeans. The armadillo must have made a lasting impression, because it is on the back of this well protected creature that the female *America* is often found in art. Prior to 1603, Flemish, Dutch, German and Italian artists used this image as a standard symbol.

The visual image of *America*, with European features, was created by European artists who never touched the soil of this hemisphere—Burgkmair, Holbein, Rubens, Tiepolo, Goya and Delacroix. Other artists adorned porcelain and silver plates, mugs and boxes with the figure of a female, native American. In 1799 Alexander von Humboldt visited Hispanic America to see what he had heard about. He wrote to his brother: "What a fabulous and extravagant country we're in! Fantastic plants, electric eels, armadillos, monkeys, parrots: and many, real, half-savage Indians...."[2] E. McClung Fleming notes, "The American image as the Indian Princess of the American colonies can perhaps best be understood in terms of three overlapping themes which are found in the allegorical situations in which she is depicted. These are her daughter-mother relationship to Britannia, her pursuit of liberty, and her command of the strategic factor of overseas trade."[3]

Between 1765 and 1783 the female symbol of America denoted the thirteen colonies. The symbol of a horse throwing the rider was introduced, but short-lived. Following the Treaty of Paris in 1783, the Indian Princess became identified with the sovereignty of the United States. As Fleming notes, this stage was superceded as "the Indian Princess gradually was metamorphosed into a Greek Goddess."[4] Later, masculine figures were introduced to symbolize America. Brother Jonathan and Uncle Sam are such examples. America was somewhat slow to adopt symbols and symbolic terms, "just as it was slow to see itself as an independent unity. In fact, it tended to be a unity in the eyes of the Europeans before it had a clear image of itself."[5]

The first American artist to adopt the image of a female Indian as a decorative device was Paul Revere (fig. 2). Other American artists followed this practice, but envisioned this figure as less barbarous. On occasion a flag was added to the figure; the Sons of Liberty were at her back; and a liberty cap and pole were included. Ultimately, *America, Columbia, Liberty*—she answered to many names—as a non-Indian female, replaced the native, American female.

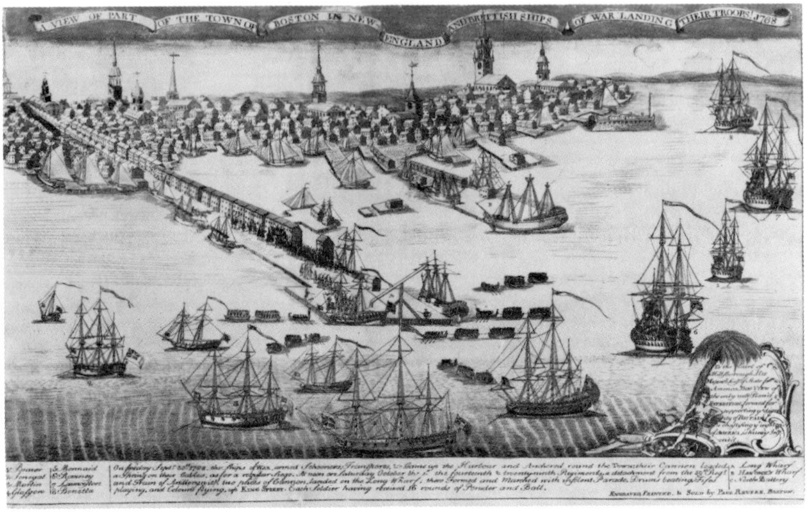

2

As stated earlier, by 1792 the eagle took its place as the iconographic symbol of the United States. Nevertheless, the Indian Princess, who unofficially symbolized America, shared Dupré's Diplomatic Medal with the eagle (fig. 3). Although dated 1776, this presentation medal was struck in Paris between 1790 and 1792. This design contributed to the vocabulary of American coins and currency. Charles Barber made a copy of the Dupré medal. Cornelius Vermeule, in his *Numismatic Art in America*, wrote, "The 'Indian Queen' is that curious mixture of noble savage and seated Artemis

3

which the French Rococo could concoct out of a nymph by Francois Boucher (1703-1770) and a vague understanding of what went on among the native inhabitants of the New World.Grass skirt and feathered headgear hardly belong with Roman throne, himation, footstool, cornucopia, classical quiver, and the svelte figure of Mercury, god of commerce."[6] Ancient Athens and Rome employed personifications of deities and images of ***Liberty, Justice***, to name just two examples that remain as decorative devices on money, as well as the images of their patron goddesses, Athena and Roma. Therefore it was logical to adorn the paper money of the United States with dozens of different portrayals of the Indian Princess.

Another Dupré medal, presented to Daniel Morgan for the victory at the battle of Cowpens on January 17, 1781, bears another version of the Indian Queen in which she places a wreath on the head of Morgan (fig. 4). This particular illustrated version, with the un-Indianlike crown, was adopted by James B. Longacre for his $1 and $3 gold pieces. A similar image appears on bank notes, both federal and obsolete.

4

To reiterate, though the eagle had official status, the feathered figure was forced to share the spotlight with the female with feathers in her hair well into the nineteenth century. As a decorative subject, "Miss America" adorned everything from bows of boats and bank notes to porcelain and playing cards (fig. 5).

These images of America, notwithstanding, were all inaccurate; female Indians, regardless of tribe, never wore feathers. In many tribes it was seldom that male Indians wore more than three

5

feathers—more often, none. Only for celebrations or important gatherings were the magnificent headdresses worn by Indian chiefs.

Therefore, it is appropriate that a native, often female American represent this land; homelands are often expressed in feminine terms. In the United States for over 100 years a female Indian symbolized America, from an earlier and therefore a longer period in Europe. As the country was developed, the Indians were shoved into convenient corners, only to be relocated when oil and other minerals were discovered on their reservations. Just as the native American was displaced from the American consciousness, so too was the image of the *Indian Princess* displaced. Now, both the image of a female, native American that represented America and the bank notes on which she once held a prominent position are both obsolete.

[1] Hugh Honour, *The Euopean Vision of America* (Cleveland, 1975), p. 1.

[2] Honour (above, n. 1), p. 11.

[3] E. McClung Fleming, "The American Image as Indian Princess, 1765-1783," *Winterthur Portfolio II* (Winterthur, 1965), p. 74.

[4] Fleming (above, n. 3), p. 64.

[5] Joshua C. Taylor, *America as Art* (New York, 1976), p. 4.

[6] Cornelius Vermeule, *Numismatic Art in America* (Cambridge, MA, 1971), p. 13.

The 'Indian Princess' on Bank Notes

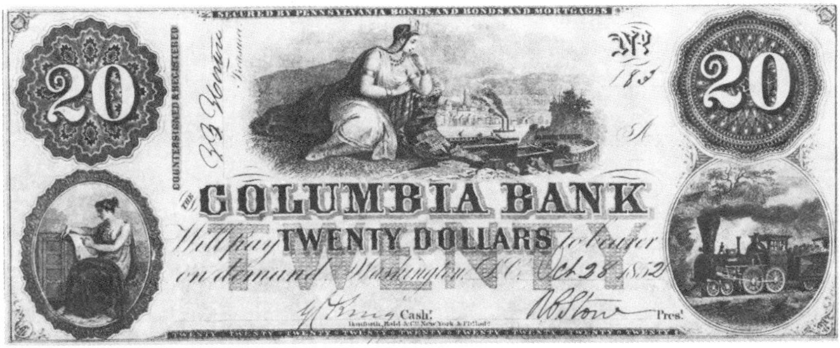

6. Washington DC. Columbia Bank, $20. October 28, 1852.

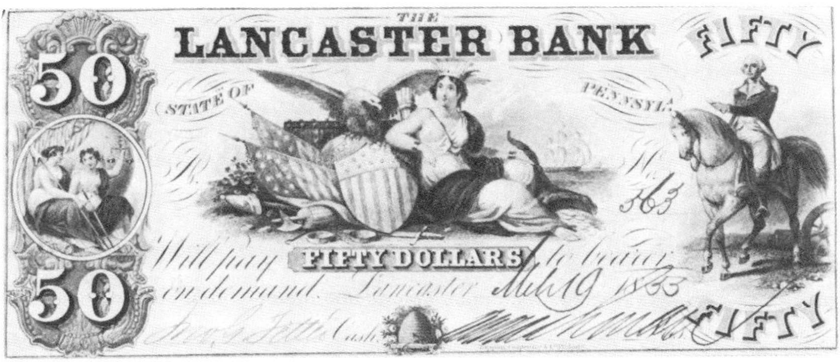

7. Lancaster, PA. Lancaster Bank, $50. March 19, 1855.

8. Egg Harbor City, NJ. Egg Harbor Bank, $1. July 1, 1861.

9. Dalton, GA. Bank of Whitfield, $2. January 1, 1860.

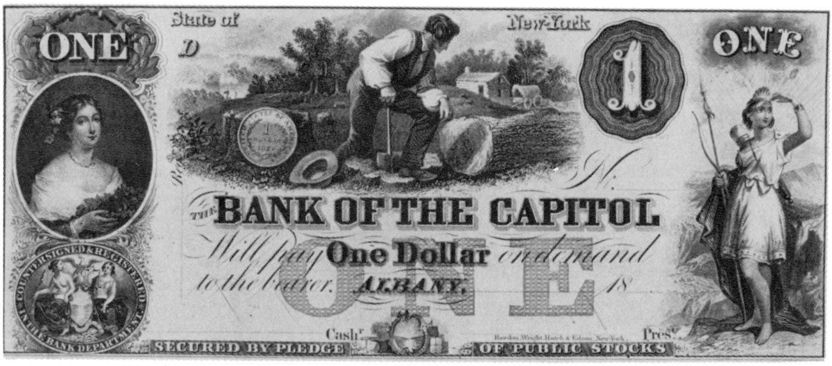

10. Albany, NY. Bank of the Capitol, $1. Proof.

The Smillie Family: Bank Note Artists

Glenn E. Jackson, DDS

Coinage of the Americas Conference
at The American Numismatic Society, New York

The most prominent family of bank note engravers during the Broken Bank Note period was undoubtedly the Smillies. James, head of the clan, was born in Edinburgh, Scotland, in 1807 to David Smillie, a silversmith. By the age of fourteen James had already served a two-year apprenticeship in Edinburgh, first as a silversmith and later as a picture engraver.

In 1821 David Smillie and family set sail for America, settling in Quebec City, Canada. In 1829 James traveled to New York in search of work and, finding numerous opportunities there, moved his family to New York in 1831.

James was an historical and pictoral engraver. He never engraved portraits but instead had another engraver fill in the figures. Fig. 1 depicts the partly completed vignette "Franklin" telling the youth in his lap about Washington with the space for the figures characteristically left blank. Fig. 2 shows the completed vignette.

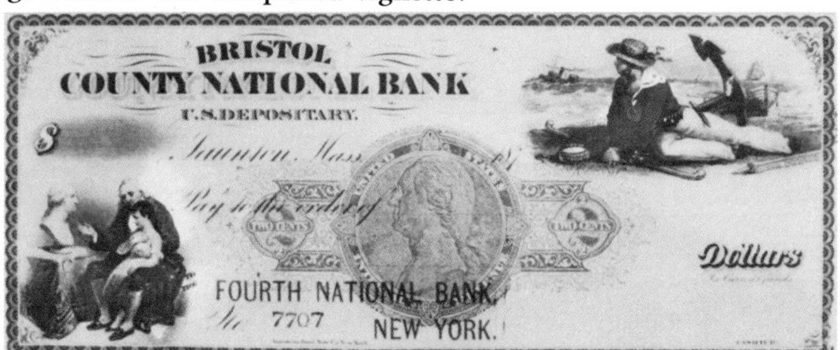

The vignette proof of Catlin's Bull Buffalo is signed but as it appears on the State Bank of Illinois $2.50 note, it is minus James Smillie's name, which was apparently lost in transferring the imprint from the die to the plate (fig. 3). Some question the buffalo's eyes but in nature they converge in a manner somewhat peculiar. It is said that the buffalo can focus on a single blade of prairie grass.

James Smillie had four sons. At one time he, along with his sons William Main, a letter engraver, and James D., a picture engraver, all worked together for the American Bank Note Co. Another son, George H., was a watercolorist. He was a member of the American Watercolor Society and served as its treasurer for four years. Little is known regarding the activities of the fourth Smillie son, David.

Signed Vignettes

The Canal Bank $100 note has as its central vignette the scene of cotton bales being unloaded from a river steamer. Below and to the left is the name James Smillie (fig. 4). The same scene appears in the lower left of the $20 note of the Farmers and Exchange Bank of Charleston, except that the corner is trimmed and the name of James Smillie is lost (fig. 5).

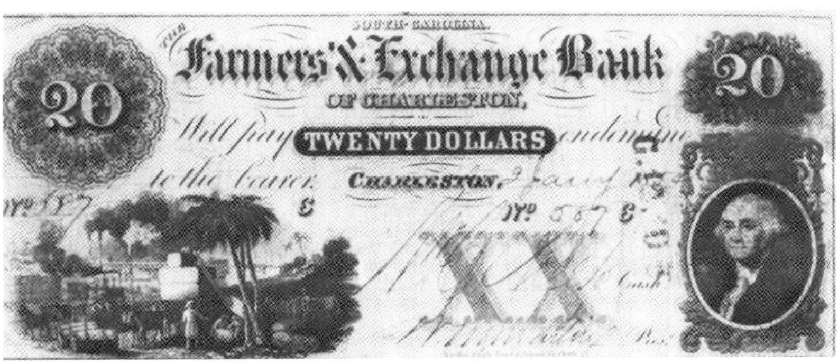

James's most famous vignette is called "The Crossing" and is the central portion of a larger vignette, "The Station." "The Crossing" omits a portion of both ends including the station. As found on the North Western Bank note of Warren, PA, it is a pastoral scene with

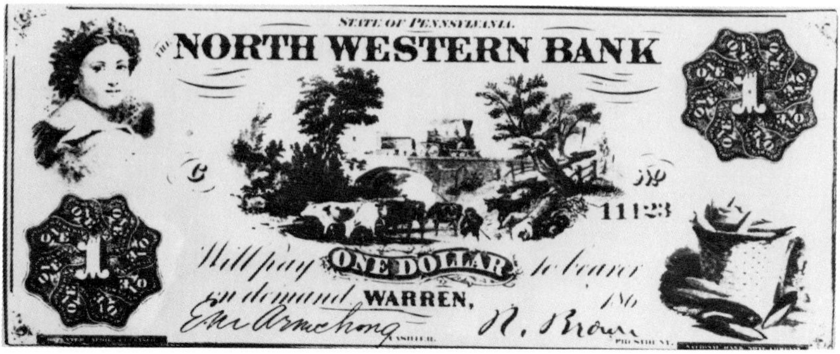

a lad herding cattle (fig. 6). After crossing the railroad tracks the cattle enter a brook, above which is a train. This same design in a much smaller size is found on the 3 cent U.S. Postage Stamp of 1869. Both were produced by the National Bank Note Co.

James's last engraving, before his death in 1885, was "The Lions at Home" after a painting by Rosa Bonheur; it depicts a lion and lioness with their two cubs. The vignette appeared on the Banco de Londres, Mexico 500 peso note, produced by the American Bank Note Co (fig. 7).

James D. Smillie was a very gifted picture engraver and artist and I think aware of what was happening to his father's signature on many engravings. He overcame this cropping of the artist's identification by placing his initials and many times the date in the body of the vignette in many subtle ways. In the case of a vignette of three deer, which was used on a check of the Third National Bank of Cincinnati, his initials and date are included in the foreground (fig. 8). Another example appears on a $2 note of the State of South Carolina

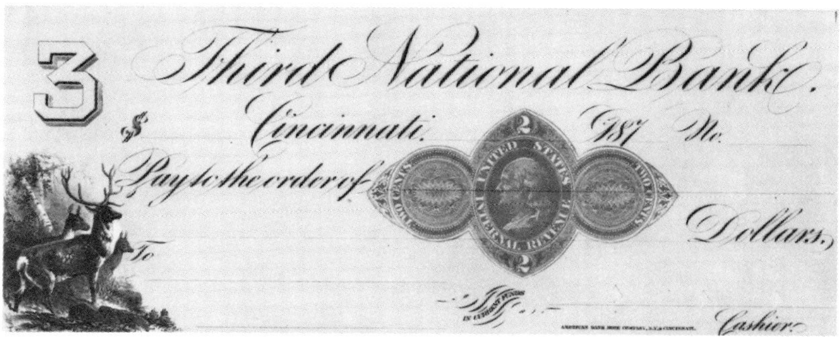

with a harbor scene as its central vignette. "J.D.S." appears emblazoned on a flag atop the ship's mainmast (fig. 9). Finally, a most interesting example is a Brantford Sault Ste. Marie, Canada $4 note (fig. 10). A sign on the building gives the name of the establishment as "J.D.SMIL."

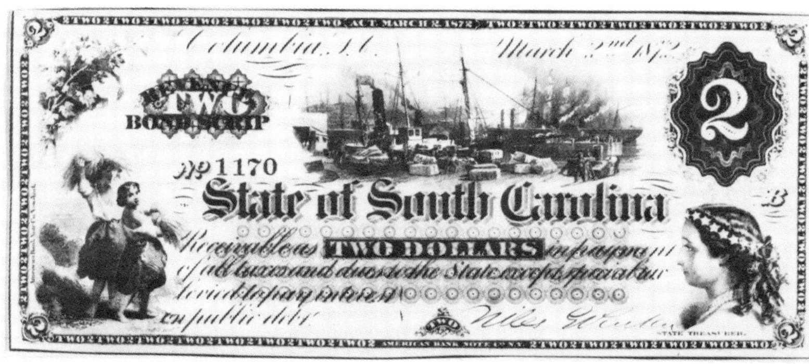

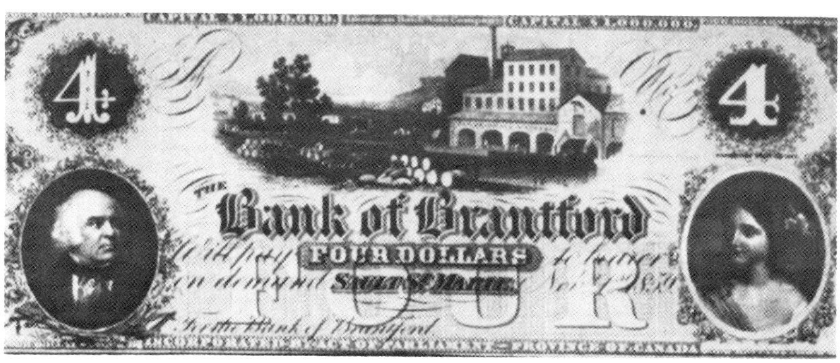

New York City Small Change Bills of 1814-1816

Eric P. Newman

Coinage of the Americas Conference
at The American Numismatic Society, New York

DeWitt Clinton, Mayor of the Corporation of the City of New York, announced to its Common Council on August 29, 1814 "that there was at present existing in this City a great pressure for small change" and he urged "the issuing by this Corporation of notes of small amount to obviate this difficulty."[1] The silver and copper coins which customarily were used by the public in the markets and stores had been withdrawn from circulation by merchants and banks because of uncertainties arising by the continuation of the War of 1812. Accordingly a sum of $5,000 in small change notes was authorized, backed by the faith and credit of the Corporation of the City of New York, the highest denomination not to exceed 12 1/2 cents. On September 12, 1814, John Pintard was selected to sign the bills, and the amount was increased from $5,000 to $25,000 with denominations of 25 and 50 cents also approved.

Andrew Maverick of the New York City copper plate printing family tried to obtain the contract to print the money, but did not succeed. This was probably because William A. Mercein, a printer at 101 Gold Street in New York City, was a member of the family of Comptroller Thomas R. Mercein, a biscuit baker at 93 Gold Street. T. & W. Mercein combined to print the first issue dated September 12, 1814, and several later issues, operating at the 93 Gold Street address. Such printing contracts are today referred to tactfully as conflicts of interest. William A. Mercein continued alone as a printer at the 93 Gold Street address for many years afterward.

The circulation of small change bills was so successful and well accepted by the public that the Common Council approved $25,000 more on November 21, 1814, and another $50,000 on December 26, 1814, raising the total to $100,000 by the end of the year. This was just the beginning.

With denominations ranging from 1 cent to 75 cents, one-half million bills had to be printed, cut apart and signed. On December 26, 1814, Thomas Franklin was authorized to join John Pintard in signing the bills. At the same time a fund for the redemption of the bills was created; the fund to be added to as bills were issued and to be invested by the Finance Committee and the Comptroller in interest bearing securities (see figs. 1-2).

The wear and tear on small change bills used by the public primarily in the food markets was substantial. The dirt from handling grain, produce, poultry, animals and meat, the conduct of business on unpaved streets in snow and rain, and the stuffing of small paper money into pockets of buyers and sellers resulted in the money rapidly becoming dirty, torn, unreadable or worn out. Within two and a half months after the bills were first authorized, arrangements were

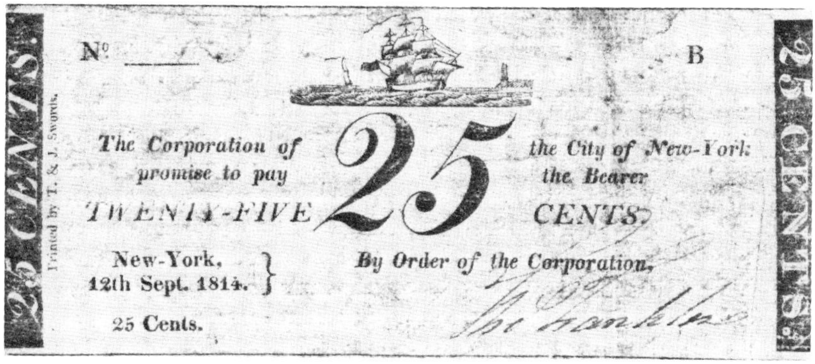

1. September 12,1814. *Thomas Franklin*. Swords printer.

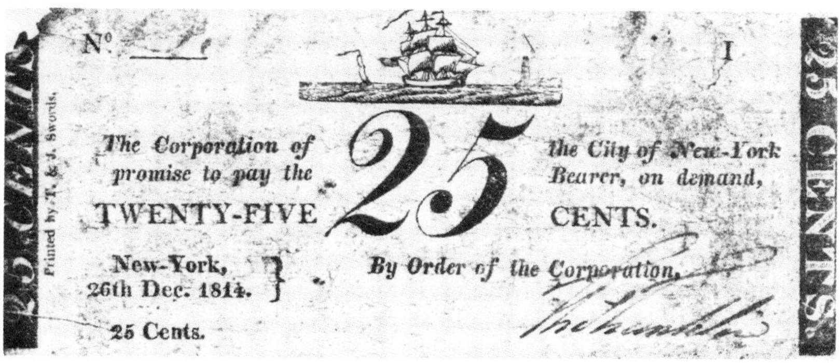

2. December 26, 1814. *Thomas Franklin*. Mercein printer.

approved for the city to receive worn out bills and to cancel them. The condition in which the known examples of bills are usually found attests to the difficulty of keeping reasonably clean, undamaged bills in circulation.

The enabling legislation did not specify what denominations were to be issued. The original August 29, 1814 authorization contained an upper limit of 12 1/2 cents and resulted in bills being printed in denominations of 1, 2, 4, 6, 9 and 12 1/2 cents on thick brownish paper, the dimensions being about 2 1/2 inches wide and 2 inches high. These denominations had no plate letters or numbering. Backs were printed only on the 4, 6, 9 and 12 1/2 cent denominations. The denominations of 12 1/2 cents and below are first dated

December 26, 1814. Bills of 25, 50 and 75 cent denominations had been issued dated September 12, 1814, which was the date of authorization of the 25 and 50 cent bills, but the 75 cent bill was not mentioned in the Council minutes until November 20, 1815, which was over one year after the 75 cent bills were in circulation. Whether this omission of authorization was an error in transcription is unimportant as no one complained. The bills of 25, 50 and 75 cents were printed on bank note paper and were about 5 inches wide and 2 1/4 inches high. They had blank backs and contained both a printed plate number and a handwritten serial number. All denominations of bills were signed by hand in ink by an authorized signer, of which there were eventually four.

The denominations on bills of 12 1/2 cents or less are printed vertically on each side of the face of the bill, reading upward on the left side and downward on the right side. For this vertical portion each denomination has a different type font. Only 9 and 12 1/2 cent bills have denominations printed on their backs.

The printers named on the small change bills were T. & W. Mercein, 93 Gold Street; T. & J. Swords, 180 Pearl Street; and J. M., 25 Van Dam Street, all of New York City. The only identification of J. M. located in New York City directories of the period is "Miller, John, carpenter, 25 Van Dam." The known plate letters on the bills of 25 to 75 cents range from A to S (including Dd) so that a substantial number must have been printed on one sheet. The observed printed dates on small change bills are September 12, 1814; December 26, 1814; July 3, 1815; January 3, 1816; and July 1, 1816. The size of the 12 1/2 cent and under denominations of the July 1, 1816 issue is slightly smaller than the size of prior similar issues, being about 2 3/8 by 1 5/8 inches and the layout of the text also differs slightly from prior issues.

Until more bills are located, a variety classification may not be as complete as desirable. In the *Catalogue of the New York State Library, 1856* (Albany, 1857), which included its extensive paper money holdings (destroyed by fire in 1911), only one New York City bill of the War of 1812 period, a 12 1/2 cent of July 3, 1815, was listed. Bills with denominations from 4 to 12 1/2 cents are known only with issue dates of December 26, 1814, July 3, 1815, and July 1, 1816, while bills of 25 to 75 cents are known for the five dates heretofore mentioned. The 1 and 2 cent bills are known only with the December 26, 1814 date. However when two bills were printed with the same denomination and the same date the principal variations are noted at the end of this article for denominations from 4 to 12 1/2 cents.

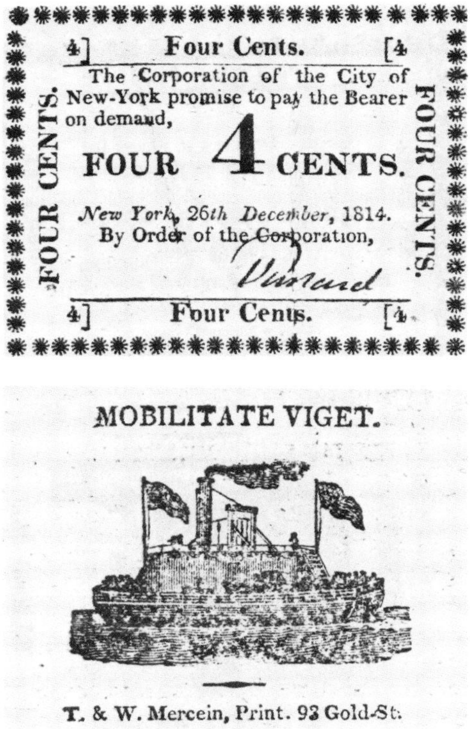

3. December 26, 1814. *John Pintard*. Mercein printer.

The Decorative Backs

The insignia and mottoes on the backs of the small size notes of 4 to 12 1/2 cents are true "folk art."

The development of steam navigation on the Hudson River is featured on the back of the 4 cent bills with an illustration of a steamboat and the motto MOBILITATE VIGET (It thrives through speed); see fig. 3.

On the back of the 6 cent bills there is a sundial with the word FUGIO (time flies) and the advice MIND YOUR BUSINESS (fig. 4). This was a continuation of the popular rebus Benjamin Franklin had created for the 1776 fractional dollar issue of Continental Currency and had been reused on the tin 1776 Continental Currency Dollar, the copper U.S. 1787 Fugio cent, etc.

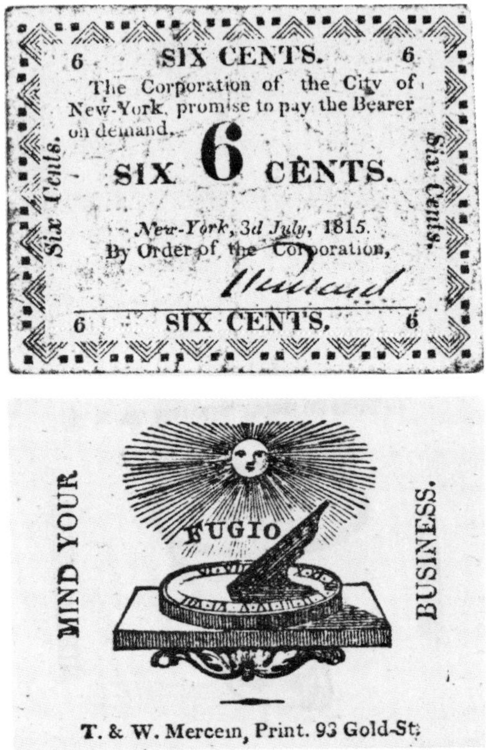

4. July 3, 1815. *John Pintard*. Mercein printer.

On the back of the 9 cent bills a compass drawing a circle around 9/100 used a decimal insignia. The motto KEEP WITHIN COMPASS is a typical "Poor Richard" style pun which Franklin would have enjoyed (fig.5).

On the back of the 12 1/2 cent bills, the figure of Hope sits abandoned on a rock in the sea, accompanied by the motto NEVER DESPAIR, an adaptation of the mythological story of Prometheus, which served as a symbol of encouragement to a nation suffering losses in the War of 1812 (fig. 6).

Unconstitutionality

The issuance of paper money by the Corporation of the City of New York was a violation of the Constitution of the United States which under Article I, Section 10, provides that "No state shall...emit

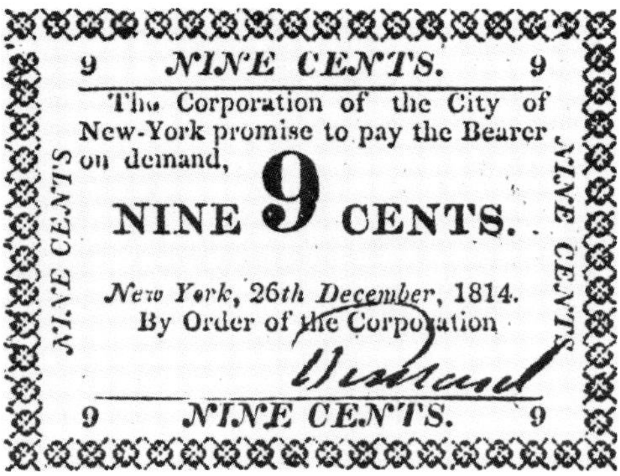

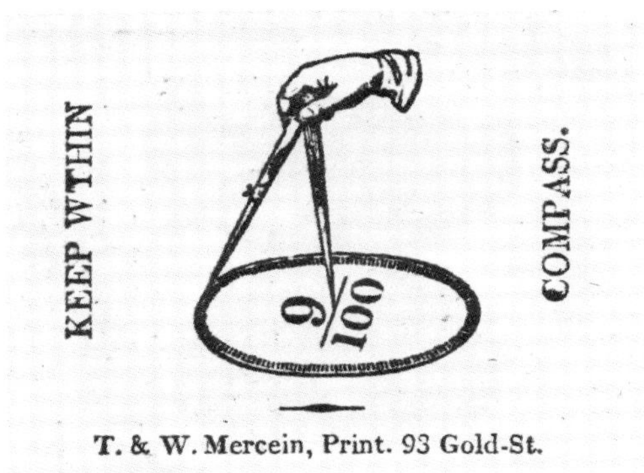

5. December 26, 1814. *John Pintard.* Mercein printer.

bills of credit.'' Small change notes are bills of credit. Although the language was not specific as to cities, this prohibition by interpretation included any political subdivision of a state. Neither New York City nor other cities considered themselves restricted by that language. In New York State, municipalities such as Albany, Amsterdam, Cooperstown, Hudson, Pleasant Valley, Troy and Utica also issued small change bills during the War of 1812 period. Apparently North Carolina as a state was also not concerned with the problem in the 1814-1823 period and issued small change notes without being formally challenged. It was not until 1824 that the Supreme Court of the United States, in the case of Craig versus Missouri, declared unconstitutional an 1821 Missouri paper money issue of notes in denominations ranging from 50 cents up to $10.

Someone might have tried to avoid the legal question of the New York City bills by changing the text of the obligation printed on

6. July 1, 1816. *William H. Bunn*. Swords printer.

the issue from a corporate promise to a personal promise. All bills dated through July 3, 1815 read "The Corporation of the City of New York promise to pay bearer..." whereas the January 3, 1816 issue reads, "In Corporation bills of the City of New York I promise to pay bearer...." However the language of the promise returned to its original text on the July 1, 1816 bills (see figs. 7-8).

The habit of issuing notes primarily for less than $1 in denomination was continued by cities and counties during emergencies in the 1837 panic as well as during the Civil War. The principal reasons that can be adduced for the failure to raise a constitutional issue were that the paper money was small change; a bona fide emergency existed; a redemption was planned when the emergency was over; there was no legal tender problem; and merchants, banks, businesses and private individuals were not prevented from circulating paper money for small change by any Federal law nor in many cases by any state law. The public authorities adopted a very liberal attitude in not enforcing laws prohibiting small change notes in emergencies.

New York City had issued small change paper money in 1790, and followed that precedent in 1814-1816 and again in 1862.

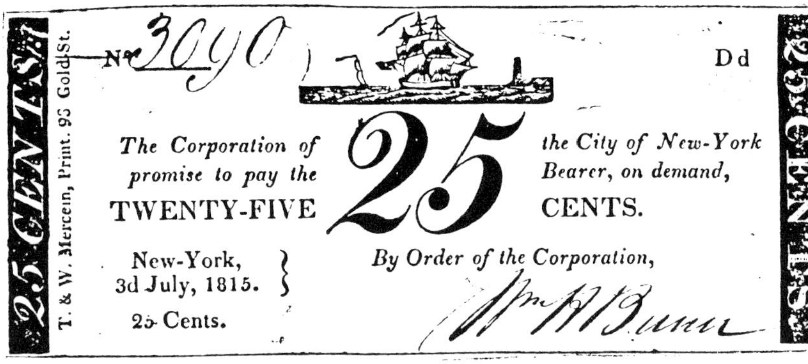

7. July 3, 1815. *William H. Bunn*. Mercein printer.

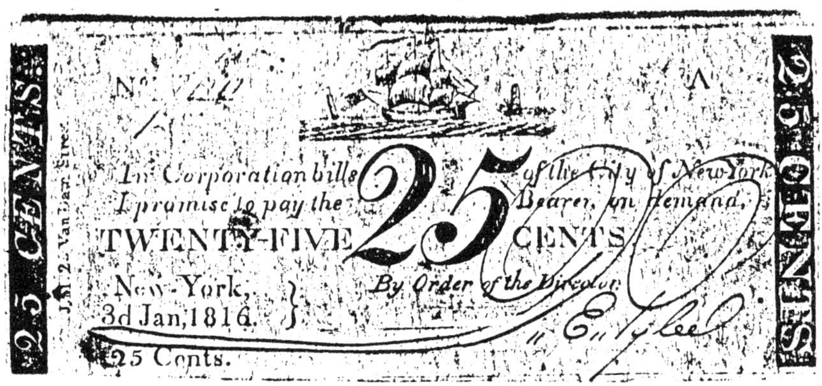

8. January 3, 1816. *Daniel E. Tylee*. J.M. (John Miller) printer.

Selection of Denominations

The money of account shilling in 1814 was still the basis for most low price transactions in New York City and was equivalent to one-eighth of a Spanish Milled Dollar or 1 real or 12 1/2 cents. Although the United States monetary unit of cents was used on the small bills issued by the city, the denominations of most bills varied from normal denominations of U. S. coins in the federal decimal system. The reason for the variation was because the New York money of account shilling and its fractions were customary for small mercantile transactions in 1814. The fact that 4 cents was equivalent to one-third of a shilling or 4 pence, that 6 cents was equivalent to one-half of a shilling or 6 pence and that 9 cents was equivalent to three-fourths of a shilling or 9 pence shows that small mercantile transactions were usually not in decimal amounts.

It appears from the extreme scarcity of 1 cent and 2 cent New York small change notes that these were issued in small quantities further indicating that the denominations of 4, 6, 9 and 12 /2 cents were the principal ones printed for the group of bills of 12 1/2 cents and under.

One obvious and curious problem of this note issue is the opportunity of the money handler to profit by shrewd payment and exchange practices. Anyone could gather a 12 cent total of the smaller denominations and either change them for shilling demominations (12 1/2 cents) or spend them for a shilling. A seller making change for a 12 1/2 cent note would give out the lower denominations as change. In any such transaction the profit would be 4 percent on each such occasion. One would double his money in 25 transactions involving 1 shilling each. There is a curious indication of this possibility on the 12 1/2 cent bills in that the fifth line reads "Twelve 12 1/2 Cents," putting the 1/2 cent only in the figures but not in the lettered text.

The Error Sheet

What apparently is the first known sheet of genuine small change bills of New York City has recently come to light and is dated December 26, 1814. It was not cut apart for circulation because a mistake was made in printing it. It consists of 12 notes, there being 2 at 4 cents, 4 at 6 cents, 2 at 9 cents and 4 at 12 1/2 cents. The total value is $1. There are six face impressions on the left side and 6 backs on the right side of each printed surface. It was intended that after printing one surface the sheet would be rotated on its long axis and printed from the same form on the other surface. This would place the faces of the notes opposite their respective backs. In the error sheet the rotation was made on the short axis, resulting in the faces being opposite upside down faces of different denominations and the backs being opposite upside down backs of different designs. Two nails in the printing form bed, protruding upward near each end of the long axis, were used to pierce the paper sheet on the first impression so that registry would take place when the sheet

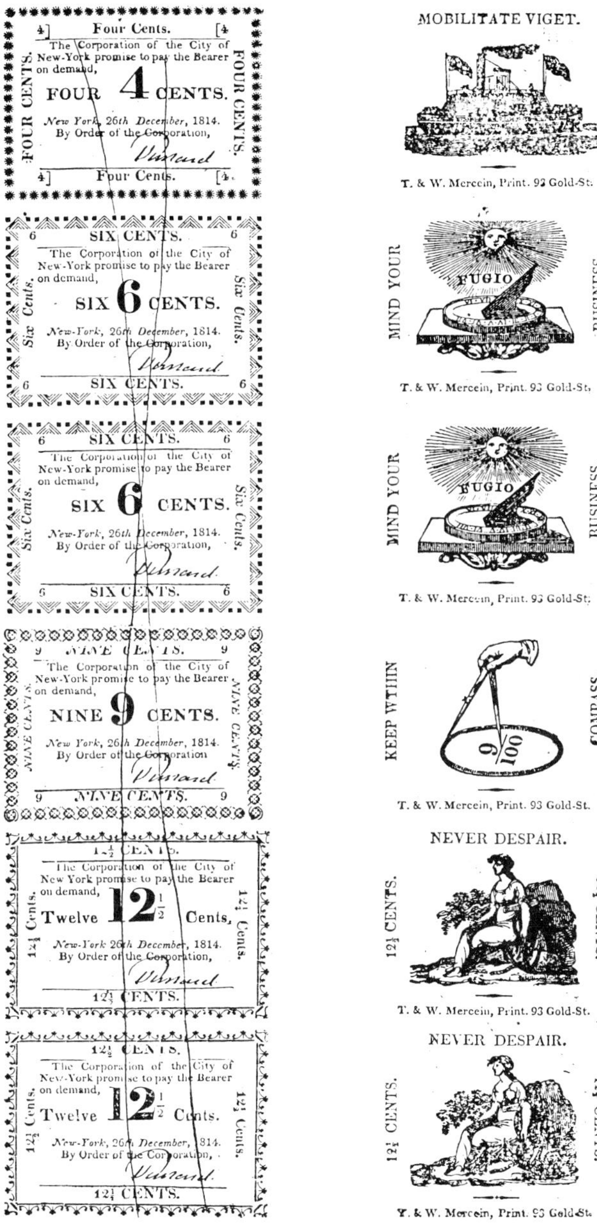

9. Error Sheet of the December 26, 1814 issue.

was rotated and fitted over the nails for the second impression. Although the nail holes were in proper position on the error sheet they cannot prevent a rotation of the sheet on its short axis which is what occurred in the printing of the error sheet.

The error was obviously discovered by John Pintard himself when he was signing a stack of sheets. He had signed all six notes on the left side of one surface and then turned over the sheet on its long axis to sign the other six notes. We can imagine his surprise when the notes he expected to sign were not on the left side but were upside down on the right side. He must have then realized something was wrong and did not sign the notes on the second side, but inked a large X on each surface and retained the sheet. It was found in his estate papers (fig. 9).

John Pintard had participated in the issuance and redemption of the 1 penny, 2 penny and 3 penny notes of the Corporation of the City of New York, having prepared the Plan and submitted it to the Common Council on February 26, 1790, and was appointed one of the committee of three to put the Plan in effect, to procure paper and superintend the printing. These earlier small change notes had solved the copper coin crisis at that time and his availability in 1814 made him the man to help solve the then existing silver and copper coin crisis. Between those periods coin circulation was active, but it is curious that in 1812 the Dutch Church at Flat Bush in Kings County found in its treasury (probably from church collection basket proceeds) $10.73 in New York City notes of 1790; the Common Council approved the redemption and destruction of these "Corporation tickets" on September 14, 1812.

A "Poor" Excuse

On November 14, 1814, it was announced to the Common Council that distresses brought on by the War of 1812 would cause applications for charity to increase substantially. This was true and by July 31, 1815, a new Alms House at Belleview was needed. The $40,000 cost of the new building was unavailable and a masterful money maneuver took place. The treasurer did not have the money because insufficient taxes had been collected. It was explained that borrowing from banks would result in interest expense for the city, but if the redemption fund for the small change notes could be dipped into, the interest could be saved and the money repaid to the redemption fund at such time or times as the small change notes were presented for redemption. The comptroller realized that "this may be in some measure considered a deviation from the Plan" of redemption security. Actually it was a simple misappropriation of the sinking fund securing the paper money. To make it appear more palatable the redemption fund of the city was to be paid interest on the borrowing. This was not a simple transfer of funds, since the Common Council had no moral right to strip the fund but by a vote of 9 to 5 approved this unusual financing measure. When it came to paying out the $40,000 it appears that the city paid out the sum in small change notes and put nothing in the redemption fund. The city took care of the poor with a poor excuse.

Unlaundered Embezzled Money

On July 15, 1816, the Finance Committee appointed William H. Bunn to sign some of the low denomination bills. He found this position quite lucrative (fig. 10). At a secret meeting of the Common Council on March 27, 1820, two "dirty" matters were brought up. First was the sale of the privilege of gathering horse manure from the streets of New York and second was the report that Bunn had undertaken to put dirty money back in circulation for his own benefit after it had been turned in for cancellation. Instead of laundering money he found he could use the small money in unlaundered form. When the amount embezzled was not restored, the secrecy was lifted and prosecution authorized. In January 1822, the accounts presented to the Common Council show that Bunn had paid toward settlement the insignificant sum of $14.37.

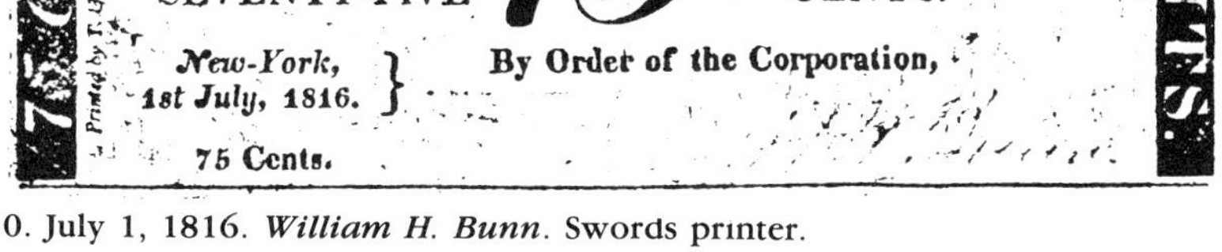

10. July 1, 1816. *William H. Bunn.* Swords printer.

Administration

The tedious work of signing, redeeming and cancelling bills was the basis for special compensation. John Pintard, on January 25,

1815, was paid $2,536.36 for cancelling bills and William McNeil $1,000. On March 15, 1815, $3,000 was paid to Daniel E. Tylee and John Bloodgood for exchanging worn out bills. On April 3, 1815, a payment of 1/4 cent for signing each bill was established, 1/4 cent for numbering each bill and $2 per day for cancelling bills.

On May 8, 1815, $20,000 more bills were approved by a vote of 8 to 4, indicating some continuing opposition to their issuance. The banks of New York City continued to urge further issues until the suspension of specie payments by the banks could be lifted and found it "essentially convenient" to have the city increase the emission another $30,000 on July 3, 1815, the total then reaching $150,000. Tylee was appointed as a signer on November 20, 1815, followed by Bunn. Although redemption of bills had taken place on a modest, yet continual basis, the total emission reached $250,000 by the July 15, 1816 authorization with the amount cancelled by May 30, 1816, being $81, 895.20. By March 10, 1817, the outstanding total had dropped to $68,716.17. When the banks resumed specie payments on July 7, 1817, the difficulty was over and by February 5, 1821, the circulation was down to an estimated $5,000. These figures indicate that the number of bills put into circulation must have been well over one million pieces, an enormous number to be printed, signed and accounted for.

The sale of U. S. securities to meet redemption requirements had been successful and interest had been earned on those securities for the intervening years. Thus the bills constituted a free loan by the public to the city and solved a monetary crisis at the same time.

Counterfeiting

Rufus King, in a letter from London dated February 14, 1799, to Richard Varick, Mayor of New York City, anticipated the counterfeiting of the bills of 1814. King had just uncovered the source of the counterfeits of the 1790 New York City issue and gave his advice as to the future by saying, "I wish that this new proof of the risque as well as injustice of these small paper money Schemes may operate to discourage us from resorting to them—the Corporation would have detected and refused to pay these counterfeits, but the Citizens, and that class of them the least able to bear the loss, would have been the sufferers." The advice either went unheeded in 1814 or probably was not remembered.

On January 25, 1815, the records show that $50 was paid to J. Hays for detecting counterfeit small change bills. These were reported by Abraham G. Forbes to be in circulation in Mt. Pleasant.

How many counterfeit bills were redeemed cannot be determined but on January 5, 1824, the approved redemption of $12.50 of them is recorded.

Only one example of a counterfeit has been located; not surprisingly, of the highest denomination issued, being a 75 cent bill dated December 26, 1814 (fig. 11). It is lithographed rather than type set. In the first use of the word Corporation the letter o becomes successively smaller. In the second use of the word Corporation the center o is smaller than the other two. This variation would not take place with type from the same font. The signature of John Pintard is forged and the name of the printer is so irregular that the printer of the genuine notes should have reason to complain about the insulting quality of printing in that portion particularly.

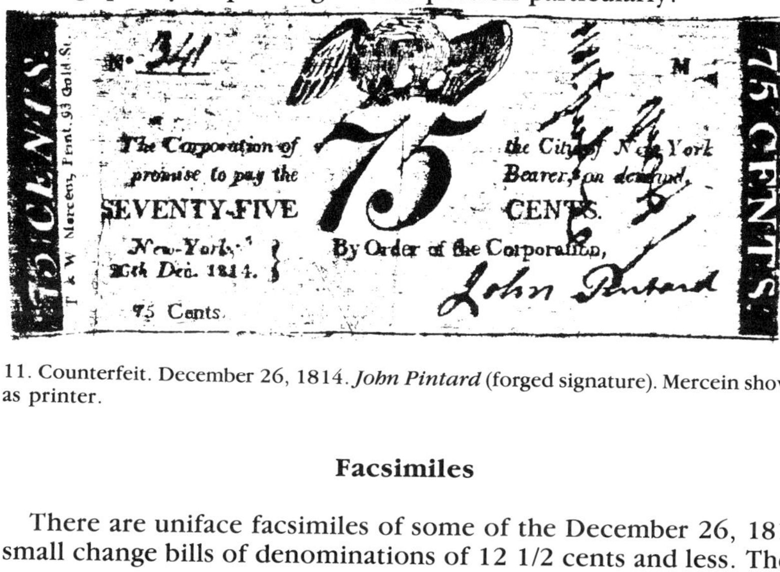

11. Counterfeit. December 26, 1814. *John Pintard* (forged signature). Mercein shown as printer.

Facsimiles

There are uniface facsimiles of some of the December 26, 1814 small change bills of denominations of 12 1/2 cents and less. They are not reprints from the original printing form which was a combination of set type and ornaments. Therefore the facsimiles should not be technically referred to as "reprints" as they have been previously. One style of facsimile was made by lithography, the entire image being drawn on a lithographic stone. This can be readily noticed by the lack of uniformity in the size and shape of the lettering. The faces of the 1, 4, 6, 9 and 12 1/2 cent denominations and the backs of the 4, 6, 9 and 12 1/2 cent denominations were made on one stone. No facsimiles of the 2, 25, 50 and 75 cent pieces were made. The nine facsimiles were printed on one side of one sheet which was folded and included as an illustration in David T. Valen-

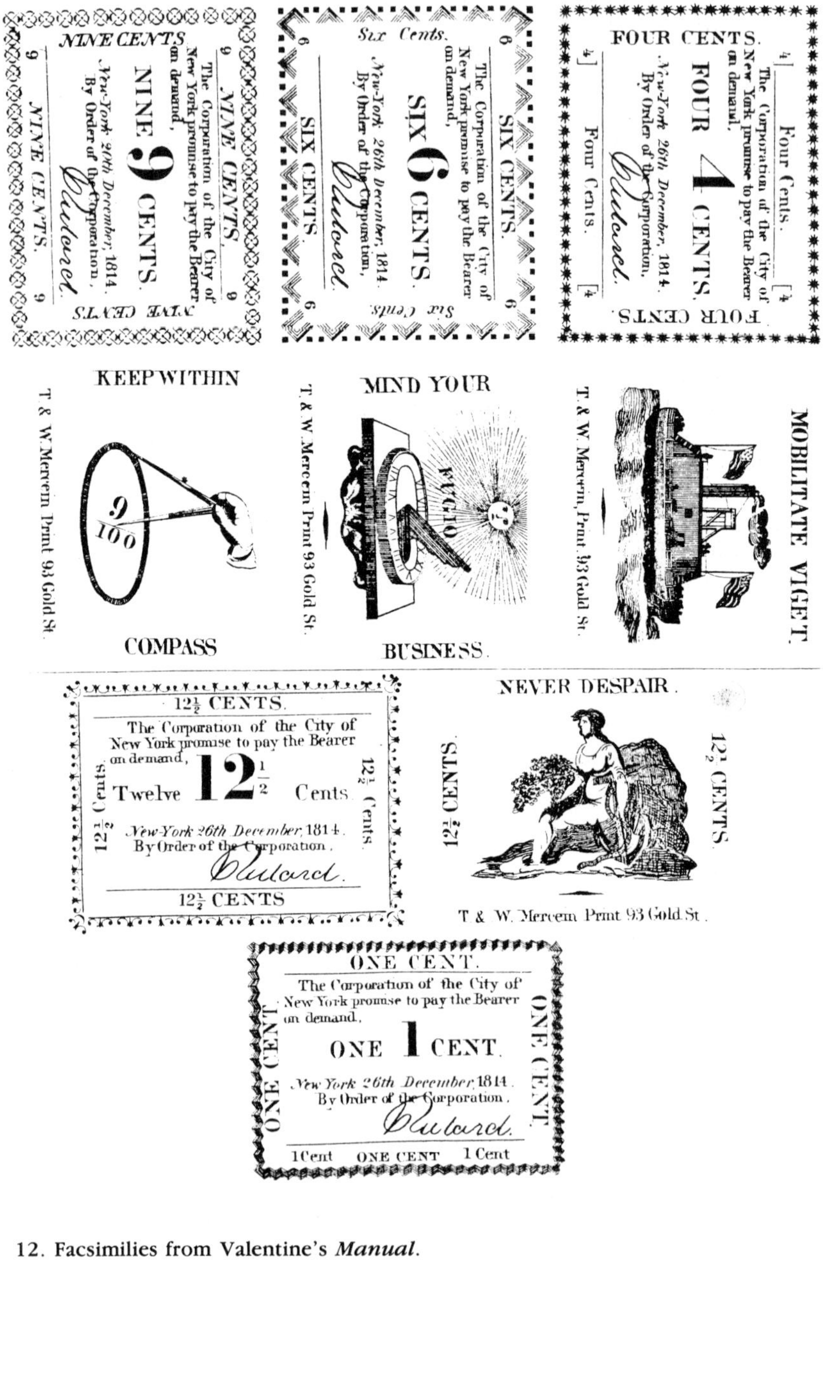

12. Facsimilies from Valentine's *Manual*.

tine's *Manual of the Common Council of the City of New York* for 1863 following page 170 (see fig. 12). The insertion is without comment or index reference. This sheet is on very thin opaque paper and not on bank note paper, the written signature Pintard is part of the lithograph and is not in ink as on the genuine bills. Many facsimiles of this type are in collectors' hands and have been removed from these manuals and individually trimmed to be single bills. The faces of some have been pasted to the corresponding backs of others in an effort to make the combination appear to be other than a facsimile.

All of these facsimiles were photographed and converted into printed illustrations in Berthold Fernow's contribution to *The Memorial History of the City of New York*.[2] However, there is no mention or reference to the New York City small change bills of 1814-1816 themselves, only to the facsimiles. These illustrations are the same size as the first facsimiles and can be readily distinguished from the genuine bills or the first facsimiles because those seen have unrelated language printed on their verso and are on wood pulp paper.

Another style of facsimile was apparently prepared only for book illustration; it is set entirely in type and has a newly-drawn back decoration. These are distinguished by use of the name John Pintard instead of only the last name Pintard as on the genuine bills. Also, the name is set either in script or other style of type instead of being a copy of his signature. There are also border decorations which differ from the genuine bills and different numbers of those decorations and the size differs somewhat from the genuine.[3]

Prior Numismatic Comment

The prior numismatic comments about New York City's 1814-1816 small change notes begin with a comedy of errors and continues it. *The Numismatist* for September 1926 quoted a then current article in the *Philadelphia Public Ledger* written by an author using the nom de plume "Mann Hatton."[4] This item gives the size of the notes as 4 inches wide and 2 1/2 inches high, which dimensions do not apply to either size of the New York City notes. The denominations cited are incomplete. The paper described as bank note paper is wrong as to notes of 12 1/2 cents or less. The notes are said not to be numbered and this is wrong as to notes of 25 cents or more. The wrong back design is described for some of the 4 cent notes. A motto is misquoted. The date of the discontinuance of the issue is wrong. The editor, in an added comment,[5] tried to correct the size as if they were all of one size and compounds the error by inserting illustrations of the uniface facsimiles (called reprints) as if they were originals. The editor did correct properly the misquotation and the erroneous back design. Farran Zerbe, in a note published in the November issue,[6] called attention to the uniface facsimiles as not being originals and added that the originals were printed on thick, brownish paper as used on Colonial and Continental Currency, but was apparently unaware of the bank note paper used on denominations of 25 through 75 cents.

In 1971 Howard Baron described his discovery of the source of the uniface facsimiles (called reprints) as well as the find of a few original notes.[7] He illustrated the plate of facsimiles in Valentine's *Manual* and explained some of the prior errors of which he was aware. He had not seen any notes of 25 to 75 cents and thus could not straighten out the size confusion or the paper confusion. He stated that there was no authorization for the 2 cent note he discovered and illustrated, but neglected to realize that the August 29, 1814 action only provided a maximum of 12-1/2 cents for denominations, but did not specify what denominations were to be issued. He asked that some numismatist clear up the puzzle, giving encouragement to the research and commentary included in this undertaking.

Summary

From an original authorization of $5,000 in small change bills, New York city increased that sum to almost fifty times the original amount. It had issued more notes than any other American small change paper money issuer other than the Continental Congress. In spite of counterfeiting, misprints, favoritism in contracts, unauthorized emissions, tampering with the sinking fund, embezzlement and unconstitutionality, this issue served its purpose well for over five years and was so fully redeemed that few examples remain. New York City had a major economic success in solving the small change crisis caused by the War of 1812.

The untangling of the many strands of this subject would not have been possible without the steady cooperation of a fellow numismatist and loyal New Yorker, Joseph R. Lasser. The diligent service of the staff of the Municipal Reference and Research Center of the City of New York was also essential. The cooperation of the Western Reserve Historical Society and Christian Blom is also much appreciated.

Minor Varieties of Genuine Bills of the Same Date

(Varieties are designated first by denomination and then by letter).

6 cents, December 26, 1814

Variety 6A: In the top border all triangular ornaments point upward. In the last line of type each 6 is beyond the end of the horizontal bar above.

Variety 6B: In the top border the fourth ornament from the left end is misplaced and separated. In the last line of type each 6 is under the horizontal bar above.

6 cents, July 3, 1815

Variety 6C: There is a horizontal bar under the first line of type. Otherwise the same as Variety 6B except for date.

Variety 6D: There is no horizontal bar under the first line of type; the bar came out of the printing form during production. Otherwise the same as Variety 6B except for date.

12 1/2 cents, December 26, 1814

Variety 12 1/2A: The first New York has no hyphen dividing it. The second New York has no comma following it.

Variety 12 1/2B: The first New York has a hyphen dividing it. The second New York has a comma following it.

Endnotes

1 *Minutes of the Common Council of the City of New York*, 19 vols. (New York, 1917). Citations relating to Small Change Bills are as follows: Feb. 26, 1790; Mar. 4, 1790; Oct. 4, 1791; Sept. 14, 1812; Oct. 12, 1812; Aug. 29, 1814; Sept. 12, 1814;

Nov. 14, 1814; Nov. 21, 1814; Dec. 12, 1814; Dec. 26, 1814; Jan. 9, 1815; Jan. 23, 1815; Feb. 6, 1815; Mar. 6, 1815; Apr. 3, 1815; May 8, 1815; July 3, 1815; July 31, 1815; Nov. 20, 1815; Jan. 3, 1816; July 1, 1816; July 15, 1816; Sept. 26, 1816; Oct. 7, 1816; Oct. 21, 1816; Nov. 18, 1816; Dec. 16, 1816; Mar. 3, 1817; Mar. 10, 1817; Mar. 31, 1817; Jan. 10, 1820; Mar. 27, 1820; Apr. 3, 1820; Apr. 17, 1820; Feb. 5, 1821; Jan. 7, 1822; Jan. 15, 1822; Jan. 6, 1823; Jan. 13, 1823; Jan. 5, 1824; Jan. 19, 1824 and Mar. 26, 1827. See also Analytical Index.

2 Berthold Fernow, "Coins and Currency of New York," in James G. Wilson, ed, *The Memorial History of the City of New York*, vol. 4 (New York, 1893), pp. 297-343. The illustrations occur at pp. 329-33.

3 An example of this style of facsimile can be found in Martha J. Lamb, *History of the City of New York*, vol. 2 (New York, 1881), p. 648.

4 *The Numismatist* 1926, pp. 476-77.

5 *The Numismatist* 1926, p. 477.

6 *The Numimismatist* 1926, p. 631.

7 "New York City Scrip of the War of 1812 Period," *Paper Money* 1971, pp. 108-10.

Currency in Crisis: America's Money, 1830-1845

Robert Vlack

Coinage of the Americas Conference at The American Numismatic Society, New York

In order to appreciate the years 1830 to 1845, it might be prudent to briefly review the series of events from the establishment of the "First Bank" leading up to what could be called the most turbulent era in our history in terms of banking and the politics involved.

First Bank of the United States

Alexander Hamilton, Secretary of the Treasury, having observed the successful financial operations of the government and of the Banks of North America, New York and Massachusetts, which all together held the entire banking capital of the country before 1791, recommended the establishment of a government bank in his famous report of 1790 on the country's finances. The Bank of the United States was given dubious legal status by an "Act of Congress" on February 25, 1791, and is referred to as the "First Bank" with a life of 20 years (1791-1911). It was capitalized at 10 million dollars, of which the government subscribed 2 million in specie and 6 million in stock of the United States at $400 per share. Because the measure was very popular, the shares of the Bank rose by 25 and then 45 percent and paid an average dividend of 8 1/2 percent on capital. Notes issued by the Bank were given legal status for all debts due to the United States, including import duties.

While the principal bank was established in Philadelphia, it soon opened branches in several major cities and states with no legal testing of the constitutionality of these banks. The foundation upon which Hamilton based the Bank was the deep-rooted conviction that society would be governed by the landed aristocracy.

In 1808, three years before the charter would expire, application was made to Congress for its renewal. It was during this First Bank era that local banks increased in number. They became favorites of the people since they furnished business facilities that were of great importance to the commercial community. This local bank interest combined to prevent a renewal of the charter of the United States Bank on various grounds, including that its constitutionality was in question; that too much stock was owned by foreign governments (mainly Great Britain) and that the local banks better served the public. Though the Secretary of the Treasury favored the recharter, nothing was done by Congress until a few weeks before the time when the Bank would cease to exist. The bill for its recharter was defeated by Vice-President of the Senate, George Clinton's casting vote, and the Bank ceased its business, returning the stockholders 8 1/2 percent premium over par value. Virtually all of the circulating notes of the Bank were fully redeemed. Most notes that have survived are either proof notes, altered notes raising the value of the notes and not redeemed because of the alteration, or more often than not, counterfeits. Most of the counterfeits were cancelled across the face with X's indicating rejection by a bank (fig. 1). During this First Bank period, the foreign debt had been paid, and for all intents and purposes, the Bank had proven successful.

1

Second Bank of the United States

By the time of the closing of the First Bank, many banks were flourishing with the ability to issue paper money which underwrote and stimulated the expansion of enterprise. Banking privileges, previously guarded by the aristocracy, were extended liberally through state legislation, especially in the period during and following the War of 1812. Wildcat money appeared, and while this may not have been the most reliable form of capital, it was accepted, since the turnover was quick, and merchants, whether rich or poor, preferred a ready flowing supply of money, however imperfect, to none. After the War of 1812, the country witnessed the usual postwar optimism and overextension of credit at an accelerated pace. By 1815 the local banks were forced to suspend specie payments leaving little other than the now-depreciated bank notes. So chaotic was the sudden change of events that it became an important argument in 1816 toward establishing a second charter of the Bank of the United States. The initial effort to establish this charter had been vetoed by President Madison in January of 1815, but now received his willing signature. Again, the charter was for 20 years, capitalized at 35 million dollars, of which the United States subscribed 7 million with the remaining 28 million to be provided by individuals (fig. 2). The creation of the Second Bank compelled the state banks to resume specie payments or close their doors. Many were aided in resumption by the new Bank, but many others, after

2

struggling on their own, were forced to cease operations.

From its inception the Bank itself indulged in speculation. Ignoring the danger signs, the directors waited too long to curb what lay ahead. By 1818 the branch banks would no longer accept any currency except their own, and presented for payment all drafts on state banks. The banks also cancelled the renewal of all personal loans and mortgages. By 1819 it was too late to stop a major depression. The west was hardest hit from the sale of lands as specie flowed east, leaving in its wake bankrupcy and a large debtor population.

This period also saw the beginning of the industralization of the northern and middle states and with it the further separation between the aristocracy and the working class. By 1820 the crisis which now had begun to abate in the east only worsened in the west. Under pressure many states passed legislation allowing state banks to issue millions in paper currency, but, rather than provide relief, this only created more inflation. The situation became so dramatic that creditors were avoiding debtors, the latter very anxious to pay off their obligations with the worthless paper currency.

From 1820 to 1824, during his second term as President, James Monroe did little to help the west and south. Land values in the west dropped as did crop values in the south, and banks not under the auspices of the Second Bank struggled, most failing within a short period of time. In the Second Bank were deposited the funds of the government, the use of which gave the bank great facilities for discounting, thus aiding the commercial community. By now, it also controlled the monetary affairs of the country. Small businessmen in increasing numbers lost ownership of their means of production. Others in the business community lost direct contact with the market.

It was felt that the victory of John Quincy Adams in 1824 would give the business community its last chance. If his administration could solve the problems of the discontent, the leadership of the commercial class would be unchallenged and the so-called American System with the Bank, tariffs, and internal improvements, would remain secure. For all his abilities, Adams, as President, showed little evidence of leadership. His inability in the face of crises convinced his peers that there was something drastically wrong in the administration of the government. His defeat in 1828 resulted directly from his failure to meet the problems of widespread discord among the people.

Jackson and the Bank War

But now the time was right and the stage was set. The multitude wanted a hero, someone who could align himself with the common man, and not be a tool of the aristocracy. Andrew Jackson's stand against the Second Bank won the approval of the people resulting in an overwhelming victory against Henry Clay who had long been an advocate of the Bank. The campaign itself was a degrading exercise with mudslinging and exaggerated accusations erupting from both Jackson and Clay factions. Jackson knew even then that his biggest fight would be against the Bank and its supporters. In his first annual message to Congress in December 1829, President Jackson took a strong stand against the renewal of the second charter of the United States Bank, due to expire in 1836. He argued that the Bank had failed to establish a uniform and sound currency for the entire nation, and that such an institution was not fully authorized by the Constitution. During 1830 and 1831, he continued to attack the Bank and renew these objections.

At the close of 1831, officials of the Bank petitioned for the first time for the renewal of the charter. The petition was presented to the Senate on January 9, 1832, and on March 13, a select committee reported in favor of renewing the charter for 15 years. A long debate ensued, and finally a bill, instigated by Henry Clay and supported by John Calhoun, passed both houses of Congress in July 1832.

On July 10 Jackson, giving expression to his strong convictions, vetoed the bill. The main emphasis fell, first, against the Bank as unconstitutional, and then, on the political argument that the Bank represented too great a centralization of power under private control. Jackson felt that if property was controlled by banks, then banks controlled the power of the country.

Against this background, the main characters in the fight for and against the Bank can be examined. On one side were Jackson, Martin Van Buren, Thomas Benton, James K. Polk, Roger Taney, and

Jackson's most loyal supporter, Amos Kendall. For the Bank were John Calhoun, Henry Clay, Nicholas Biddle, John Quincy Adams, and finally Daniel Webster.

Nicholas Biddle, a brilliant aristocrat of cosmopolitan Philadelphia, was only 37 when he became President of the Bank of the United States in 1823. He was an active president whose judgment was widely respected, and until 1830 all his ventures succeeded. For Biddle, the Bank was an independent corporation, on a par with government, and not responsible to it except by the narrowest interpretation of the charter. Biddle attempted to strengthen this position by presenting the theory that the Bank was beyond political good and evil, unlike Alexander Hamilton who, in presenting the first charter, was clear of its intention—that the Bank was not a mere matter of private property, but a political entity of the greatest importance to the government.

Again in his annual message in December 1832, Jackson's hostility to the Bank was manifested by a recommendation to remove the public funds from its custody and sell the stock of the Bank held by the United States. This measure was brought about when the questionable conduct of the Bank in the matter of the retirement of a series of securities came under review. The Treasury had told Biddle that spring to be prepared to redeem 6 million dollars' worth of these securities on July 1. Biddle requested postponement on the grounds that disbursements would disrupt commerce. Reality revealed that Biddle had been too generous in granting loans to supporters of the Bank, and he was unable to produce the necessary funds. When it was discovered that an arrangement had been made with a London banking house to purchase several millions of these securities and withhold them from the United States government, Jackson was infuriated and declared the Bank unsafe.

Jackson felt the time had come to act. He requested an investigation into the Bank's financial conduct. Two reports were presented just before the Congress adjourned. One was a short report pronouncing the Bank as sound and recommending that the deposits be retained. A second, much longer report, gave evidence of the critical conduct of the western branches and of questionable practices by the Bank itself. However, through a timed manipulation, it was resolved that the Bank was safe and business was to be conducted as usual. Jackson, not satisfied, requested recommendations from his own staff, and based on their findings, it was decided no longer to support the Bank and to remove the deposits. Jackson instructed William Duane, then the Secretary of the Treasury, to remove all government funds from the Bank of the United States, and to deposit these funds into state banks designated by Jackson. These Banks became known as "Pet Banks" and were carefully selected by a Jackson committee as being the most sound and reliable. Duane refused to remove the funds, claiming that he was not answerable to Jackson, though he was President, but only to Congress. Jackson solved that problem by firing Duane and replacing him with Roger Taney. With that strategic move, the removal of the funds was accomplished.

This was to be the first real setback for Biddle, who began to realize that he perhaps had underrated Jackson. However, Biddle felt that this defeat would only be temporary, and he set about getting the Bank back into sound financial standing. This he accomplished by calling in loans from the west and south, creating a further hardship and scarcity of money. Biddle knew the charter still had three years to run, and if the Bank was found safe, the charter would have a good chance of being renewed, thus saving the Bank. The Pennsylvania legislature, and afterward other legislatures, recognizing the ploy, recommended the Bank of the United States not be rechartered by Congress, and government funds not be restored.

Round two was lost, but the fight was still to continue. If a sound bank did not bring Congress to renew the charter, perhaps monetary blackmail would. In July 1834, Biddle issued orders to loosen credit and allow cash to flow throughout the country. For the moment, all appeared well again. However, state and local banks could not avoid speculation and as more banks appeared on the scene, more and more paper money was issued, based only in part on the government deposits. A very significant factor in the boom was land speculation. Prices soared, and inflation affected all areas of the economy. Government lands in the west were selling as never before, and foreign speculators invested heavily with the expectation of turning high profits. Payments for the lands were made with paper money, principally from state banks, but when these notes were presented for payment by the government, they could not be redeemed in specie. Most banks, including Jackson's Pet Banks, were lending government funds on questionable security as well as circulating huge quantities of paper money with no hope of redemption. Biddle had created havoc with the economy and now tried to persuade Congress that the situation was so bad that only by rechartering the United States Bank could stability be restored. Unfortunately, by this time, no one would listen. As a result of the inflationary situation, the President was forced to issue the famous "Specie Circular," directing the receivers of public monies to accept only gold or silver specie in payment for public lands. Prices

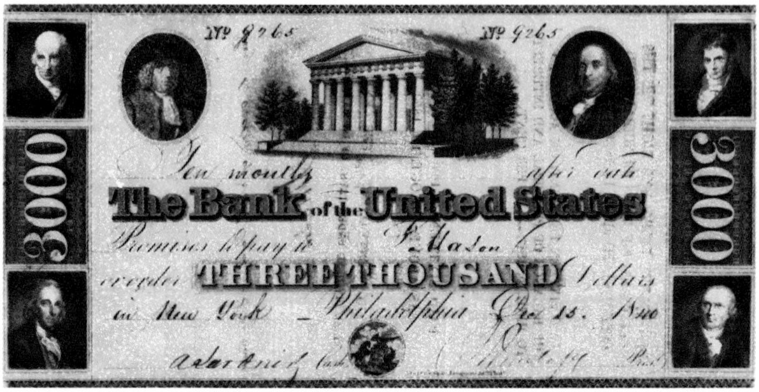

3

dropped, land speculation collapsed, and currency depreciated on a daily basis. The Bank of the United States, without a renewed charter, expired by limitation in March 1836.

Biddle would still not concede defeat. In the same year, he received a charter through the Pennsylvania legislature with the same capital, and continued to do business as the Bank of the United States of Pennsylvania. Notes issued reflected only the title "The Bank of the United States" (fig. 3). This new bank was compelled to suspend specie payments with all the local banks in 1837, again in 1839, and in February 1840, it made a final suspension with no hope of recovery and closed up its affairs. The entire capital was spent, there remained nothing for stockholders, and the Bank was considered bankrupt; widespread distress was the consequence. Biddle resigned, his Bank owing other banks over 7.5 million dollars.

Biddle himself, after defeat on top of defeat, became a broken man. He was indicted on criminal charges in a city where once he had been a hero. Had he not died in 1844, and if justice had taken its turn, he would have undoubtedly spent time in the penitentiary.

Currency of the Period

Most currency issued throughout this period depreciated rapidly and finally became worthless; that which survived came from those banks with enough specie and credit support to withstand the disaster. Between 1836 and 1840, it appeared that anyone could take out loans and issue some form of paper money in denominations as low as 5 cents to 75 cents for minor transactions (fig. 4), and higher for private institutions, towns, boroughs, or cities (fig.

4

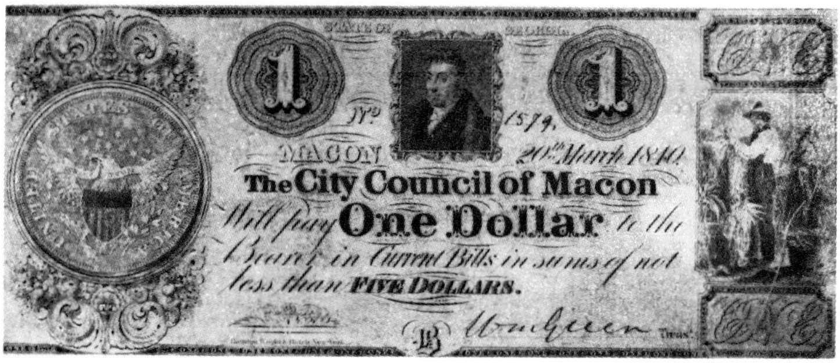

5

5).Money was also issued for the construction of canals, bridges, railroads, or other community projects (fig. 6). The worthless minor notes (later all worthless notes) were dubbed "shinplasters" contending they were more useful for treating sore shins than for purchasing goods (fig. 7). Many of the notes were made payable to such notables as Henry Clay, Daniel Webster, John Quincy Adams, Daniel Boone, and even George Washington who had little chance of redeeming them (fig. 8). Addition of these names was intended to give the currency added credibility in the mind of the unsuspecting receiver of the notes. As banks failed, forgers would cleverly alter the failed bank's name and location with the name of a bank still

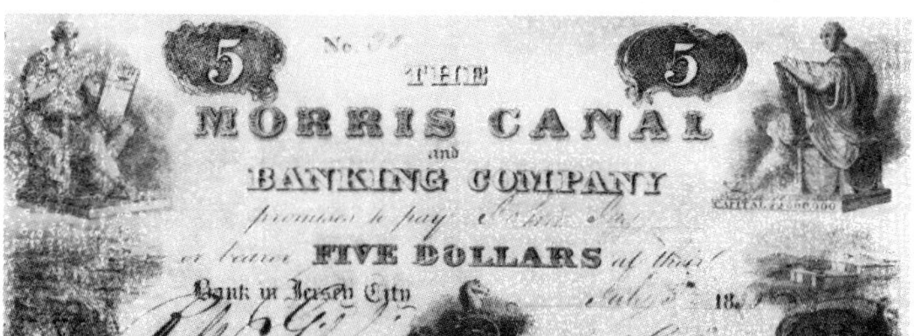

6

7

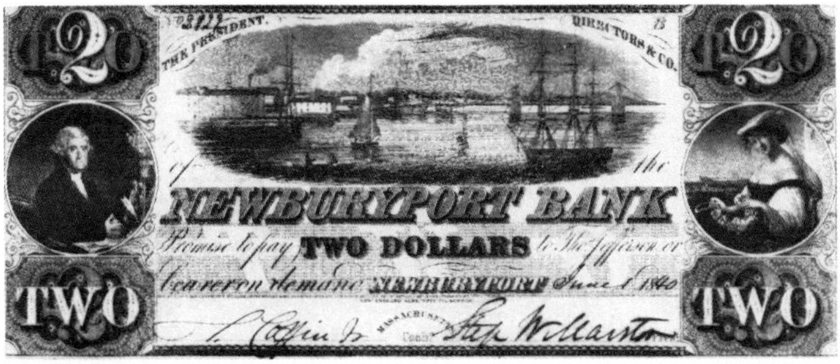

8

9

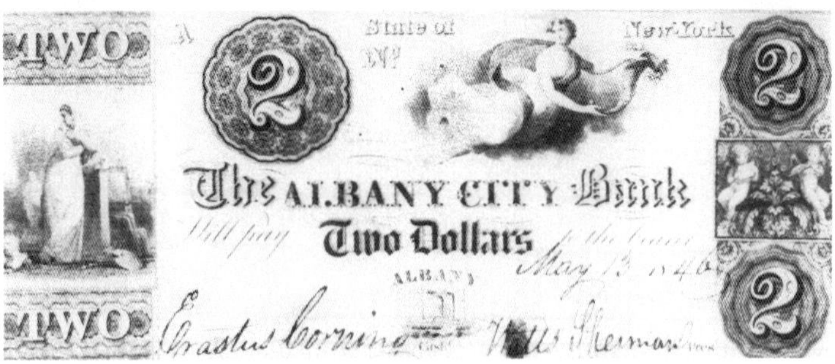

9 (altered)

in operation (fig. 9). Spurious notes were issued on banks that never existed, but whose names did not appear on counterfeit detectors distributed to banks on a continuing basis (fig. 10). If a name did not appear on a counterfeit detector listing, it could conceivably be accepted, at whatever discount.

Many satirical notes were also issued by the pro-bank supporters denouncing and ridiculing Jackson and his followers. they were issued under the titles "The Glory Bank," the "Humbug Glory Bank," or the "Kitchen Cabinet Bank" referring to Jackson's closest advisors and supporters, not necessarily members of his cabinet (fig. 11).

10

11

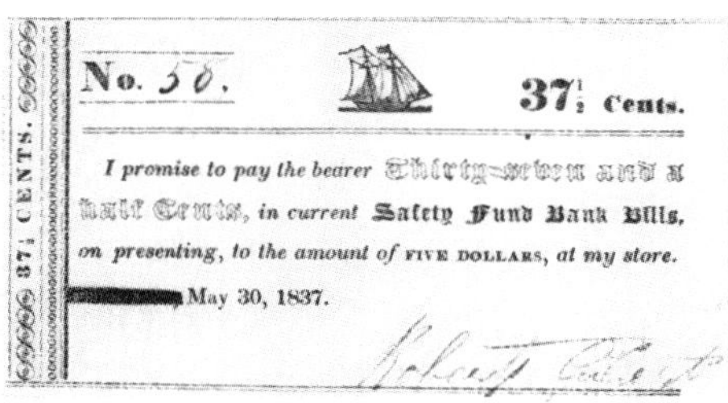

12

Notes were also issued by merchants, payable at the issuing store, and there exist today literally thousands of varieties of these notes (fig. 12). These are referred to as merchant scrip and we may never know just how many varieties exist, since so many are one of a kind and dispersed widely in private collections.

Tokens were also issued throughout this period, some for want of specie of any sort, and are referred to as merchants' tokens; other tokens denounced Jackson and the policies that followed throughout his term in office as well as the policies of Benton and Van Buren. These are characterized as Hard Times Tokens, and much has been done recently in this field which had remained dormant among the collecting fraternity for many years.

The Independent Treasury

On March 4, 1837, Martin Van Buren was inaugurated President. Though he was not as popular as Jackson, his principles were the same, and with the endorsement of Jackson, he was elected to office in a country deep in financial frustration. Business and banking communities came down hard on Van Buren to repeal the Specie Circular, but Van Buren stood firm and would not yield to the pressures. On May 10, 1837, the New York banks suspended specie payments, followed by banks throughout the country. Something had to be done and done soon. The restoration of the Bank of the United States was out of the question, and continued support of the state banks at this point was likewise futile. The idea of an independent treasury was proposed as early as 1829 under the title of "Separation of State and Bank," and was seriously considered by Jackson in 1833. In his 1837 message to Congress, Van Buren called for this "Independent Treasury," dubbed by the opposition as a "Sub-Treasury." The President regarded the use of circulating notes of banks under the current situation as a violation of existing law, and he proposed that the Treasury should be kept by public officers and that the Bank and the State should be completely divorced. Finally, after long and continuing debate, a bill passed both Houses of Congress and was signed into law on July 4, 1840. By this action, the financial affairs of the government had once again returned to the original design of the Constitution and remained that way until the founding of the Federal Reserve System in 1913.

Throughout Van Buren's tenure, recovery was slow, too slow in fact for the working class and financial institutions as well. The divorce of Bank and State presented, for both friend and foe alike, a continuing hard money policy and with it hard times for all. By rejecting bank notes in payment for revenue, it considerably restricted the power of banks over the currency and the country. By confining banks to the needs of the commercial community, it held them to legitimate economic transactions and limited their capacity for redistributing wealth in favor of a single class. How different this new reform was from Biddle's concept.

Van Buren's policies remained loyal to those of Jackson, but when a depressed four years gave way to an outcry for change, the election of William Henry Harrison in 1840 was the result. Harrison had been elected as a figurehead whom Clay, Webster, and doubtless others had calculated could be controlled. His death soon after his inauguration installed John Tyler as the new President. Tyler submitted to the idea of repealing the Independent Treasury, but when Clay tried to push through a bill for a new bank charter, Tyler returned it with a resounding veto.

By 1842, the Bank had lost whatever glamour and prestige it once had, and even Webster, one of the most ambitious supporters of the Bank, coldly observed that the idea of a bank based upon private subscription was now obsolete.

By now the Bank War was over and other pressing problems demanded precedence. The annexation of Texas in 1845 and the controversy over slavery would soon become the topics of concern. The famous battles over the banks and monetary policies would fade into history.

Lynchburg (VA) City Paper Money of 1862

Raymond H. Williamson

Coinage of the Americas Conference at The American Numismatic Society, New York

The city of Lynchburg is located on the bank of the historic James River near the geographic center of Virginia, in sight of the Blue Ridge Mountains and a short drive from Natural Bridge, Monticello, and Appomattox Court House. In 1861, when the Civil War began, Lynchburg was a city of some 7,000 people; about half of whom were black. In the state, only Richmond, at 38,000, Petersburg, Norfolk and Portsmouth were larger. The city was named for the Quaker founder, John Lynch, who started a rope ferry across the James in 1757 and who successfully petitioned the Virginia General Assembly for a town charter there in 1786.

According to the economist, David R. Goldfield,[1] in 1859 Lynchburg had the highest per capita wealth of any city in the United States, save one—only the great whaling center of New Bedford, Massachusetts, was wealthier. Lynchburg's "per capita wealth" was skewed since the statisticians counted the city's large black population, then mostly slaves, as "wealth." The city's wealth was due mainly to the sale, warehousing and shipping of tobacco; also, Lynchburg was the traffic hub for railroads, highways and canals, and it was the shopping and communications center for a large agricultural area.

But the advent of all-out war in Virginia in 1861 vastly changed the lifestyle of the people, which earlier had been generally pleasant and slow-gaited. The wartime city became a busy center for hospitals, a marshalling yard for war material, and a rest-and-recreation area for soldiers on leave. The man in the street thought of the war as another Revolutionary War to break away from Northern oppressors, just as native sons like George Washington, Patrick Henry, Thomas Jefferson and other Virginians had broken away from Britain in 1776.

But by mid-1862, the Confederate cause seemed at low ebb. The federals had occupied Nashville in February, St. Augustine and Jacksonville in March, and had established a permanent base at New Bern, North Carolina; in May New Orleans had fallen as had Baton Rouge and Pensacola, and Memphis was lost in June. In May, Lynchburg reported 3,000 sick soldiers in improvised hospitals and the Diuguid undertaking establishment had buried 930 by September. Over 300 Yankee prisoners were held at the fair grounds.

In Virginia, as in the North, prices for everyday purchases skyrocketed and all hard money disappeared from circulation—even the small coins needed for making change. Virginia banks had stopped specie payment in March 1861. Hard money was hoarded. The only remedy to this grave problem was to issue paper money and lots of it—even "small notes" of less than a dollar for change. But

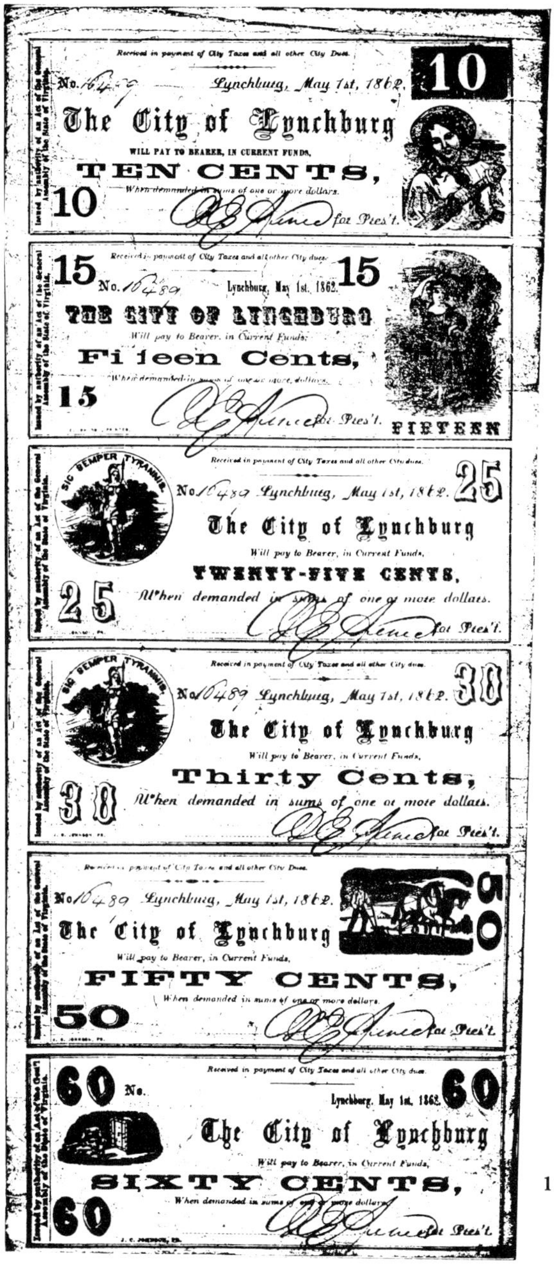
Received in payment of City Taxes and all other City Dues.
No.
Lynchburg, May 1st, 1862.
10
The City of Lynchburg
WILL PAY TO BEARER, IN CURRENT FUNDS,
TEN CENTS,
When demanded in sums of one or more dollars.
10
for Pres't.
15
15
Lynchburg, May 1st, 1862.
THE CITY OF LYNCHBURG
Will pay to Bearer, in Current Funds,
Fifteen Cents,
15
for Pres't.
FIFTEEN
SIC SEMPER TYRANNIS
Received in payment of City Taxes and all other City dues.
Lynchburg, May 1st, 1862.
25
The City of Lynchburg
Will pay to Bearer, in Current Funds,
TWENTY-FIVE CENTS,
25
When demanded in sums of one or more dollars.
for Pres't.
SIC SEMPER TYRANNIS
Received in payment of City Taxes and all other City dues.
Lynchburg, May 1st, 1862.
30
The City of Lynchburg
Will pay to Bearer, in Current Funds,
Thirty Cents,
30
When demanded in sums of one or more dollars.
for Pres't.
Lynchburg, May 1st, 1862.
50
The City of Lynchburg
Will pay to Bearer, in Current Funds,
FIFTY CENTS,
When demanded in sums of one or more dollars.
50
for Pres't.
Received in payment of City Taxes and all other City dues.
60
No.
Lynchburg, May 1st, 1862.
60
The City of Lynchburg
Will pay to Bearer, in Current Funds,
SIXTY CENTS,
When demanded in sums of one or more dollars.
60
for Pres't.

1

governing bodies everywhere were most reluctant to begin issuing paper money, doubtless because legislators remembered the horror stories which resulted from the overissues of paper money during the American Revolution less than a century earlier.

The North authorized the first federal Civil War paper money in July 1861, but the first postal currency, issued in 5-10-25-50 cent notes, was delayed until August 1862. The Confederate government authorized its first paper money in March 1861, but no note was then to be of a denomination lower than 5 dollars. The CSA government never got around to issuing really small notes; the 50-cent note was the lowest denomination issued and that not until April 1863.

The individual states of the Confederacy rather than the central government took the responsibility for issuing small change notes. Virginia's law was enacted March 29, 1862. Her cities and counties were quick to respond, a few having illegally made earlier issues to fill a desperate need. At Lynchburg, the City Council had discussed an issue of small notes as early as October 1861; denominations of 25 cents, 50 cents, $1 and $2.50 were considered, but no action was taken. However, after the Virginia small-note enabling law was passed at the end of March 1862, action at Lynchburg was very prompt. The printed date on all the notes is May 1; delivery by the printer, J.C. Johnson, began on May 6. The same day, David E. Spence, a prominent Lynchburg attorney, started signing and serially numbering the notes while the new City Treasurer, William W. Norvell, began passing sheets of them through his wicket to citizens in exchange for Confederate bills. And finally, two days later, the City Council passed the enabling law for eight denominations of the Lynchburg notes, including authorization to pay Spence for signing them.[2] The first printing of these notes was in sheets of six, one each of 10-15-25-30-50-60 cents (fig. 1). Spence signed the first 800 sheets "David E. Spence" (fig. 2); thereafter, tired of the drudgery,

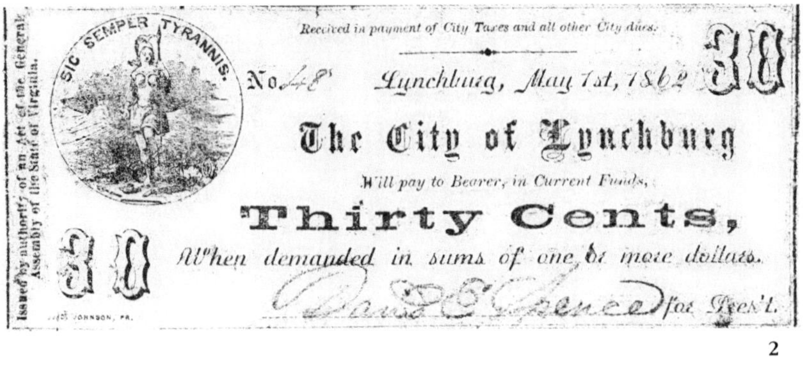

2

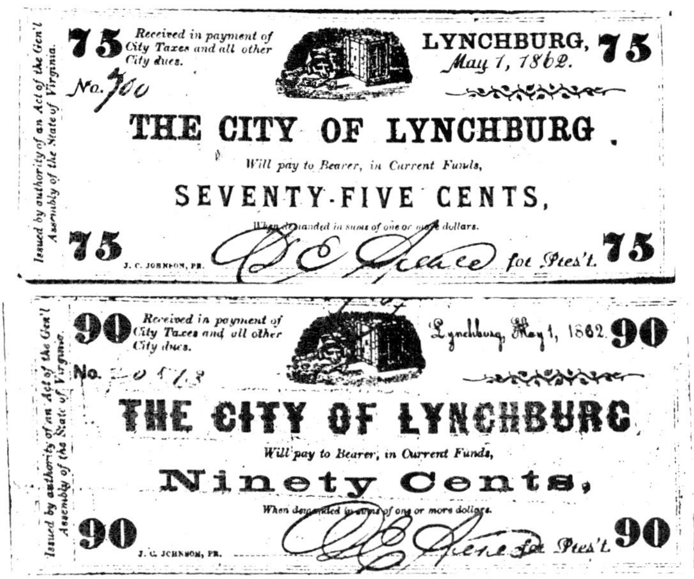

3

he shortened his signature to "D. E. Spence." A serial 796 of the long signature has been observed and serial 802 of the short signature. A little later, smaller sheets of the other two authorized denominations of notes were printed, containing one note each of 75 and 90 cents (fig. 3), all signed "D. E. Spence."[3]

It is interesting to speculate as to just how the earlier six-note sheet (total face value $1.90 each) and the later two-note sheet (total face value $1.65 each) were exchanged in May for Confederate notes—the lowest denomination of which was then $5. The sale of complete sheets, while desirable, was not mandatory. Of some help in making change may have been the first issue of Virginia $1 treasury notes in mid-May and the first issue of CSA $1 notes in June. It seems doubtful whether these $1 notes were immediately available in Lynchburg, so Treasurer Norvell must have done most of his change making with shears.

The Enabling Laws

After considerable debate and amendments, the Virginia small-note enabling act was signed into law by the Governor on March 29, 1862, effective immediately. It contained some clauses which are instructive as to the issuing philosophy of Virginians and of other

Southern states. The city of Richmond was authorized to issue city notes up to $500,000, much of which had already been issued; all other cities and towns (but not counties) having over 2,000 population, plus three smaller towns, could issue small notes under $1 up to double the state tax assessment on real and personal property. Banks were required to receive and pay out these notes, and the issuing agency must receive them in payment of all dues such as taxes, although they were not actually called "legal tender." Provided these sums were not exceeded, cities, towns (and counties) also could issue such notes to pay out money grants to arm and equip military volunteers, and to give aid to the needy families of soldiers. Quarterly reports to the Governor were required by each issuing agency to show the amount and denominations issued and outstanding. (If such reports were prepared, apparently they have not survived, except for one statewide partial summary report by the Virginia Auditor of Public Accounts dated January 1863.)

By the fall of 1863, the degree of price inflation in the Confederacy was about 15:1 in terms of gold, so that there was no longer any need for town, city or county issues of small notes under $1. Accordingly, the Virginia General Assembly passed the act of September 22, 1863, withdrawing from all these agencies the right to issue more of "any note, scrip or certificate." While this law permitted continued circulation of small notes already issued, if a note was redeemed by the issuing agency it could not be reissued. The *Lynchburg Daily Republican* for February 14, 1863, queried only nine months after issue had begun:

> What has become of them? Can anybody tell what has become of the thousands of dollars of city notes issued some time ago by the Council? We scarcely ever see one now. Can it be true, as we hear, that some parties in the city are hoarding them up, as a safer currency than Confederate Money?

The Lynchburg small-note enabling law also contains some instructive concepts. The total issue was limited to $120,000, in eight stated denominations. The notes were all to be manually signed and serially numbered by the Council President, or some other person whom the Council might appoint. The Council appointed another person by Resolution the same day—David E. Spence. The notes were to be so numbered as to indicate exactly the number of each denomination issued; the only reasonable way to do this was to have every note on a sheet bear the same serial number and, if one note need be scrapped, the entire sheet would be discarded. The exact language on the face of each note was specified, including the statement required by state law: "Received in payment of City Taxes and all other city dues." After signing, the notes were to be delivered to the City Treasurer (William W. Norvell) and only he could issue them to the public, in exchange for coin or current bankable funds; that is, CSA notes. Bookkeeping and reporting details were specified; none of these data appears to have survived. Treasurer Norvell was supposed to report at the December 1862 City Council meeting the amount of each denomination of notes he had issued; no such report has been found.

The Issues

Of the $120,000 authorized, only $72,418.60 was actually put into circulation by Norvell. Spence was to have been paid $1 per thousand notes for signing and numbering them, but was actually paid $4 per thousand—still lower than any other such payment rate of which records have been found. Since his total pay is a matter of record at $649.41 for issuing $72,418.60 in notes, and we know the total face value of each six-note sheet was $1.90 and that of each two-note sheet was $1.65, the mathematically inclined will observe that we have enough data to set up two simultaneous linear equations in two unknowns, so that we can determine the exact number of six-note and two-note sheets. Solving these equations, we find that exactly 20,171 of the six-note sheets and 20,663 of the two-note sheets passed through Treasurer Norvell's wicket. Recently recorded serial numbers on nearly 1,000 of these small notes make calculated quantities seem reasonable. The highest observed serial number from a six-note sheet is only eight less than the total; and for the two-note sheet, only 73 less than the final number.

Thus Spence signed his name 162,352 times during the hot Lynchburg summer of 1862. If he worked continuously at full speed he might sign 700 notes per hour or a note every 5.1 seconds. At this rate, he would require 29 eight-hour days for the entire run. These notes were apparently serially numbered by another hand—numbered in red ink, the same as for their predecessor notes of the American Revolutionary era.

The notes are all uniface, typeset on newsprint paper, with the same legend on each denomination. Several different standard cuts were used as seen on many other similar notes. These were: dog and safe on 60, 75 and 90-cent notes; Virginia's Great Seal on 25 and 30-cent notes; a girl on the 10-cent note; a harvest scene on the 15-cent note, and a man plowing on the 50-cent note.

Due to severe price inflation, the Lynchburg small notes went to sleep in the hands of final holders. Although no one had a trunk full, as is so often heard in the case of final holders of Confederate currency, there were some right sizable accumulations of the Lynchburg paper here and there—perhaps used by children for playing store on a rainy afternoon.

Two years and eight months after the Confederate surrender at Appomattox, one very large accumulation of Lynchburg small notes (several thousand dollars' worth) was in the hands of a respected three-member private banking house in the city, doing business under the name Miller and Franklin. This partnership, seeking any legitimate means for fiscal survival during the tribulations of Reconstruction, decided to claim the right to use their hoard of small notes to pay $1,125 in city taxes in line with the language on the face of each note: "Received in payment of city taxes and all other city dues." So that their position would seem reasonable, Miller and Franklin proposed to pay ten percent of their taxes each year in this paper for ten years. There was much difference of opinion among Council members. After hours of discussion at a Council meeting called December 6, 1867 to discuss the question, it was voted 6 to 5 to accept ten percent of taxes in the small notes of 1862, Council adjourning at 2:00 AM. Much emotional talk resulted among the citizens, the gist of which was that those who held notes applauded the decision and those who had none considered their acceptance unfair. It was contended that most of the small notes were in the hands of a few speculators who purchased them for ten or twelve cents on the dollar, and that their acceptance would not benefit the people at large, but rather only a few capitalists. The dissenting multitude likened the Lynchburg city notes to those of Virginia counties "which nobody expects ever to be paid" because the county notes were authorized by state law only to promote the war effort. The question then was: were the Lynchburg notes issued for "support of the rebellion?"

Three days later, Council met again and revoked its decision to accept the small notes. The City Tax Collector, insisting on payment "in the currency of the United States," proceeded to levy on three large iron safes in the offices of Miller and Franklin in lieu of the $1,125 taxes assessed the previous May 1, and advertised the safes to be sold December 21 at public auction. But on December 14, Miller and Franklin, refusing to pay the taxes as directed, petitioned the Circuit Court Judge at Lynchburg and secured an injunction, served on the Mayor, to prevent the selling of the office furniture. Their petition offered to pay their 1867 tax with enough 1862 small notes scaled to equal the gold value of those notes at the time of their issue—stated as $1,687.50 face value for a tax of $1,125, or 150 percent of gold value. These notes were actually filed with the petition, but were not accepted by the Tax Collector. So Miller and Franklin reluctantly proceeded to sue the City for not accepting its own notes.

The suit was brought as a case in equity in the Circuit Court at Lynchburg. The manuscript record survives today as Case No. 1792 in the files of Corporation Court. The elected City Council, as defendant in this suit, filed a reply in terms which they must have hoped would help to avoid U. S. military control of Council. However, the following May, military control came anyway with the "adjournment" of the elected Council and the substitution of a Council "appointed" by U. S. military authorities. The small-notes case came to trial July 1, 1868, and the judges decided for the defendant City, despite the plaintiff's inclusion of a deposition by City Treasurer Norvell that the city's expenses "for equipping arming and supporting volunteers &C...were made from the 'City Fund Account' and have no relation to or connexion with, the 'Small Note Account'." As defendant in the suit, the City's answer to the charges covered many legalistic aspects of the case, but the main thrust of their argument was that the only *legal* government of Virginia in 1862 was the Wheeling "reformed government," which was a part of the United States rather than of the Confederacy, and that the *illegal* government at Richmond had no right to repeal the 1860 Virginia law which banned all "small notes;" that therefore the 1862 Lynchburg notes were illegally issued in the first place; that in 1862 "the state of Virginia, and the people thereof, were in a state of open insurrection and rebellion against the government and people of the United States of America, of which the State of Virginia was a member, and the said act was passed to enable the said City Council to provide for and aid and assist those engaged in said insurrection and rebellion against the authority of the said government of the United States, to prosecute and sustain said rebellion." In copying these quoted words, the trembling hand of the ancient Clerk of Court (pretty obviously an unreconstructed rebel) shook more violently than before and the script actually ran off the paper at this point. The City's answer continued at great length, and finally, with sarcasm, stated: "And the said City, not deeply sympathizing with the misfortune of the plaintiffs, who in a spirit of rash speculation, adventured the enormous sum of sixteen dollars, as rumor says, in purchasing these notes to pay a tax of $1125, they pray that the injunction...be dissolved."

The injunction against the city was dissolved, but plaintiffs Miller and Franklin immediately appealed the case against the City to the district Court of Appeals, also at Lynchburg. The case came again to trial on December 3, 1868. This time a comprehensive printed summary was prepared by the plaintiffs, including their petition, the City's reply, several exhibits and the judgment of the first court—practically verbatim—with added material and an index, together running to 20 pages. The judges again ruled against the plaintiff bankers, who again appealed. This time, the appeal was to the highest court in the state—the Supreme Court of Appeals at Richmond. The case was tried for the final time more than three years after the start of the argument, on March 13, 1871. One of the Supreme Court judges, Francis T. Anderson, prepared a very able and lengthy summary of the case, appearing in print as some eight pages in *Grattan's Reports*, vol. 20.[4] The judge was of the "opinion that the decree of the District Court be affirmed." The other judges concurred. Thus, Miller and Franklin had at long last lost their case and presumably they paid their delinquent taxes and court costs in "currency of the United States." The firm was still in business in Lynchburg until the 1881 death of partner John M. Miller. The private bank then merged with a national bank, which (after further mergers and name changes) exists today.[5]

The 1869 year-end report of Lynchburg City Treasurer Norvell showed that the city held $6,362.15 in its "Small note account" and also in its "Cash city fund, Small note account $4,894.31." He recommended that these accounts be "charged off" and the "notes, etc. be packed in a box...separate from all other papers." Apparently at least some of the notes survived there until 1954, when on February 1 a news item appeared with pictures of some of the notes, and an offer by the Judge of Corporation Court that "persons interested in a souvenir of the city may obtain money specimens by coming to the Court House." While all eight denominations were present, "few assortments of all denominations are left...The true background of the certificates is not known, but the judge says they...are not associated with any case and are of a souvenir value only." By 1961, the Clerk of Court said that all sets and partial sets were all gone long ago. The response to "something for nothing" was tremendous.

The earliest observed catalogue listing of the eight denominations of 1862 Lynchburg city small notes is in the Scott Catalogue of 1894.[6] There may well be earlier listings, and there have been many later ones. As one would expect, the most comprehensive listing appears in Affleck's *The Obsolete Paper Money of Virginia*, where six of the denominations are pictured.[7] This excellent reference, long out of print, is soon to appear in a second edition, with additions. The notes are quite rare in uncirculated condition; no 10 or 15 cent note has been observed in this condition. Eric Newman's six-note sheet is believed unique (see fig. 1). No two-note sheet has surfaced, but its existence is proven by the straight edges at top and bottom of the sheet, and the fit at center scissors-cut of two notes, 75 cents and 90 cents, bearing identical serial numbers. A few notes appear quite frequently at coin show bourses and in paper money auctions, but rarely in top condition.

The Lynchburg Denominations

The Lynchburg small notes are of prime interest as collectibles because a set of eight denominations includes not only four expected denominations (10-25-50-75 cents), but also four odd and unexpected denominations, each a multiple of 15 cents (15-30-60-90 cents). Where else can we find so many odd denominations in a single series? There must always be a reason for the selection of such odd numbers, but City Council minutes of 1861 and 1862 do not reveal it, nor do the few surviving personal papers of Council members and others who may have been involved in the choice. However, a study of 1862 Richmond and Lynchburg newspapers made an even hundred years later yielded a surprisingly plausible reason for the odd denominations—an idea then thoroughly circumstantial and speculative but now firmly held and believed because of further supporting evidence, though still lacking contemporary documentation. The key newspaper item was an editorial in the *Richmond Whig* of January 23, 1862, which stated in part:

> A correspondent suggests a change in the denomination of our coins...as a means of removing us further from the Yankees...If we were to revert to the old English pounds, shillings and pence...we might go far to bother the Yankees and conciliate the good will of the English people...But whether or not it be deemed expedient to return to our original colonial coin, it would be very gratifying to us to see the Yankee *dollar* disappear altogether and forever from our vocabulary.

This Richmond editorial was paraphrased and quoted in many details in the *Lynchburg Virginian* two days later. Added editorial comment questioned the proposed abandonment of:

> our present system of computing money...It is (now) the work of a Southern statesman; and Jefferson deemed that he had rendered his country a signal service in

> substituting the simple federal system for the more difficult and English system of pounds, shillings, pence and farthings...Our servants understand (the present money system). They know the meaning of dollars and cents, and can comprehend readily the relation in which one stands to the other...No, if the Yankees choose to wear shoes, we need not go barefoot in order to testify our total dissent from them in principle and practice. The masculine gender among them wear britches...but we do not propose therefore to be a nation of *sans culottes*.

As a result of discovering these newspaper proposals, it seemed reasonable to review the small-change money in Virginia at the time of the American Revolution. This money was nearly all paper money rather than coins. It was a great surprise to find that the paper money denominations for small notes were 15-30-60-90 *Pence*! These small Virginia Treasury notes, issued in 1775 and 1776, were multiples of the 15-pence note, which was named on its face a *Pistereen* for the Spanish (not Spanish American) two-real piece of equal value in the Virginia monetary system of six shillings to the Spanish dollar.

It thus seemed apparent that the 1862 denominations had been chosen so that, no matter whether the Confederacy reverted to colonial pence or retained the use of Yankee cents, some of the selected denominations would be correct.

At the time in 1962, I consulted with some dozen seasoned paper money collectors, hoping to get contemporary references or opinions. While no contemporary references have as yet been located, 4 of the 12 gave qualified endorsement to the colonial-relationship idea. To test another possible explanation for the denominations, a wide search for ephemeral pricing data for common articles was made, although the quest proved very difficult, but not impossible, because prices were changing so rapidly with inflation. This research will not be reviewed here, but suffice it to say that no correlation whatsoever was found between denominations and prices—particularly prices of Confederate postage stamps, which were then available only in five-cent and ten-cent versions. Nor is there any correlation with tax rates.

It is also interesting to note that several denominations of the Virginia colonial notes of 1775 and 1776, noted earlier, were signed by a William Norvell (fig. 4). Therefore, a further attempt was made to confirm the colonial-descent concept for the denominations by developing the Norvell family genealogy. This search proved very difficult due to the lack of printed genealogies, burned court houses, and three generations of Norvells named William, plus

4

a cousin also so named. The results of this search are as follows.

Two first cousins operated on the 1862 notes: Lorenzo Norvell (1801-1880), elected to the City Council in April 1862 and appointed to the two-member Finance Committee and the three-member Small Note Committee; and William W. Norvell (1795-1871), the City Treasurer. Their grandfather was William Norvell (1746-1794), Justice of Hanover County, who today has a host of descendants in the Lynchburg area. A first cousin of this William Norvell of Hanover County was yet another William Norvell (1725-1802) of Williamsburg in James City County, who served in the colonial House of Burgesses and who was a signer of the colonial paper money; the grandfather of these two colonial Williams was Hugh Norvell (d. 1716) of James City County. This Hugh Norvell then is the common ancestor of the note signer of 1775 and the note operators of 1862.

Most old Virginia families have maintained a close kinship for many generations. Hence, it would have been normal indeed for Norvell family members in 1862 to have been familiar with the paper-money activities of grandfathers and cousins. In this case, the collateral relationship seems entirely adequate to make the colonial-descent concept of the paper money credible without further contemporary documentation. After twenty-three years, it's time to tell the available story.

So, having searched for contemporary documentation of "reasons" for the odd denominations of Lynchburg small notes without success, but having found excellent circumstantial evidence, this story will close with the words of Sherlock Holmes in *The Sign of Four*: "...when you have eliminated the impossible, whatever remains, however improbable, must be the truth."[8]

[1] David R. Goldfield, *Urban Growth in the Age of Sectionalism, Virginia, 1847-1861* (Baton Rouge, 1977), p. 201.

[2] Charles M. Blackford, ed., *General Ordinances of the City of Lynchburg* (Lynchburg, 1867), p. 211.

[3] Detailed in R.H. Williamson, "David Edley Spence, Signer of the Lynchburg Small Notes of 1862," *The Virginia Numismatist*, July 1976, pp. 47-54.

[4] Peachy R. Grattan, *Reports of Cases Decided in the Supreme Court of Appeals of Virginia, from September 1, 1870 to June 1, 1871*, vol. 20 (Richmond, 1871), pp. 330-43.

[5] The firm's motivation in pressing the court case was not only for business reasons, but also as a possible aid to many impoverished people across the state who, holding valueless Conederate money and little or no "hard money," might find a small relief if the city small notes could be spent.

[6] Scott Stamp and Coin Company, *Standard Paper Money Catalogue*, 4th ed. (New York, 1894), p. 97.

[7] Charles J. Affleck, *The Obsolete Paper Money of Virginia*, vol. 1 (Hampton, Va., 1968), pp. 84-86.

[8] In addition to those mentioned, literally dozens of people and organizations have supplied data for this study, particularly the staff of the Virginia State Library at Richmond, and Lucy Harrison Miller Baber regarding Norvell family genealogy. I am grateful to all for their help.